D1032221

B 1735 020 128 868

131

4

L S. BUCK

TELL

THE

PEOPLE

Talks with JAMES YEN about the Mass Education Movement

Two-thirds of the world's people are illiterate, ill clad, underfed, and at the mercy of disease. The Mass Education Movement is a plan, tested for thirty-odd years, to transform these millions in a generation.

UNIVERSITY
OF PITTSBURGH

LIBRARIES

5.50
100L

TELL THE PEOPLE

BUCK, PEARL S. (PEARL SYDENSTRICKER), 1892-1973.

TELL THE PEOPLE

*Talks with James Yen About
the Mass Education Movement*

by

PEARL S. BUCK

LA 1131
B8
1984

International Institute of Rural Reconstruction

Silang, Cavite The Philippines 2720

U.S. Office: 1775 Broadway
New York, N.Y. 10019

1984

COPYRIGHT, 1945, BY PEARL S. BUCK
All rights reserved. This book, or parts thereof,
must not be reproduced in any form
without permission

PUBLISHED BY ARRANGEMENT WITH

Harper & Row, Publishers, Inc.

To

the people of Tinghsien, China
who so cheerfully gave themselves
as an experiment for people everywhere

FOREWORD

IN THIS MOMENT in which we now live, between war and peace, there is no time for small or local things. All that is thought, all that is done, must be weighed for its value to the world. War has brought the nations, even the Allied nations, no closer, and division is everywhere among the governments. But a single great need makes the world a whole—the need for peace. Everywhere the peoples long for peace, that they may live.

Yet how long can there be peace? Peace cannot be made as one makes a machine or as one makes a business or even as a war is made. Peace comes only as the result of other accomplishments. There will be peace in the world only when there are equality and security everywhere for all human beings. These peace plans upon which men consume their days and brains are useless. We must first think and plan how to remove oppressions and hunger and ignorance. When people are content, there will be peace. While people are oppressed by bad governments and by ignorance and by hunger there can be no content and therefore no peace. To work for peace, as though it were a thing in itself, with no relation to causes, is the crowning folly of our foolish age.

Three fourths of the peoples of the world today are oppressed by bad government, are ignorant, are ill-fed and at the mercy of disease. Therefore the first plans ought to be made for them. How can they be taught, how made healthy, well-fed, informed and self-governing? Until some plan for this is carried out our talk of peace is senseless. Is there a plan for changing millions of people in a single generation? There is no time to wait for the long processes of education as we know it. Education must proceed through reconstruction. The people must learn while they do. While they go to school, they must rebuild.

Here is the record of a plan already at work for twenty-five years, already consciously tested for just such a problem as the world faces today. The plan was made by a Chinese and put to work for China. Twenty-five years ago James Yen and his friends saw the problem of their own country, a country where three fourths of the people were illiterate, at the mercy of disease, badly governed. They asked themselves how, in a generation, this could be changed. They set themselves to answer their own questions. War struck before the work was complete, but the tests had been made and the plan is ready to put into action, not only all over China, but everywhere. It could be of inestimable value in the southern part of the United States, in parts of South America, in Cuba and in Puerto Rico, above all perhaps in Africa, India, the countries of Southeast Asia and anywhere where there are people who are hungry and illiterate and badly governed.

But I must put first a caution. No one can carry out this plan, whether as a private individual or through government, who does not have first in his heart the belief which these young Chinese had, the belief that the plain peoples are worthy of food and health and livelihood and good government. Respect for the human being is the first requirement of any program for peace.

There is a grave danger that this requirement is forgotten in much of the thinking that is being done today, notably in the western countries. Granted goodwill and intelligence, the tendency is to base world planning on what it is thought people need instead of finding out what people want. A program imposed upon people, even for their own good, will fail if it does not fulfill what they themselves want. Compulsion, even for their own good, will simply defer the hope of peace. If people, being ignorant, want what is not for their good, then education and guidance, not compulsion, are required.

This little book contains the story of how a small group of Chinese intellectuals, moved first by admiration for the quality of their own common people, went to live with those people, learned what they wanted as well as what they needed, and how a plan was made and perfected and put into action.

Today the whole world needs such a plan. I submit it as primary for the peace.

TELL THE PEOPLE

CHAPTER ONE

James Yen was born in China forty-seven years ago, in the province of Szechwan, the son of an old scholar family, which, like all old scholar families in China, had always lived its own cultivated life. It was a life very remote from the people. Some countries have had their aristocracies of birth and some have had aristocracies of wealth, but China has for centuries had an aristocracy of scholars. It is true that individual scholars, geniuses, have risen from plain families and by their own merits have entered the aristocracy of scholarship. But these have not been the real aristocrats. They have been like the merchant barons of England, recognized for their individual achievements but not members of great aristocratic families.

The true nobility of England is the old landed families, inheritors of titles for generations. In exactly the same way did the old scholar families of China establish a sort of nobility. Tradition led them to educate their sons and even sometimes their daughters in the ancient classics, and tradition, too, taught them to think that work with the hands was beneath them and that the common man who toiled for his food and shelter was of a class different from the scholar who cultivated his mind and his manners.

Into such a family was James Yen born and he was not different from his ancestors except in the age in which he was born. It was an age when China had come into contact with the West, and it had become the fashion to educate the sons not only in the ancient Chinese learning but also in the western learning. Thus this young man, who might have lived out his life as a scholar in the tradition of his family, absorbed in books, in ancient poetry and history, was brought into the life of the new world, too. He was sent abroad to study in America.

MEN OF BITTER STRENGTH

But something more than this went into the making of James Yen. He happened to be born at a time that brought him into the first World War. Since he spoke good English and was intelligent and able, he went to France to help in welfare work for the great numbers of Chinese laborers who were there. China's real contribution to the first World War was labor. These men were "coolies," that is, men who worked by the strength of their hands and bodies.

"Coolie" is a significant word. It means literally "bitter strength." These men could neither read nor write. But they had families whom they loved and they wanted to write to their families. They went to this young Chinese intellectual who was in charge of them and asked him to write for them.

Before long James Yen learned to respect these men of bitter strength. He had never known them in his own country. They had belonged to a different class there. They were workmen and he was a scholar. Without thinking very much about it he had accepted the difference in position at home. But here in democratic France, symbolically, and in a war which was being fought for democracy, he came to know the common men of his own faraway country. He found them ignorant and helpless when it came to expressing themselves on paper, but he knew by watching them that actually they were strong and resourceful and able with their hands. That they could not read and write was no fault of their own. They had never had a chance to learn, for there had been none to teach them.

As he wrote down for them the messages which they wanted to send to their families, he came to see that though these men were illiterate they were not really ignorant. They thought shrewdly and profoundly, they understood, with a sort of practical common sense, the things they saw around them in France, they had lively humor and warm hearts. They were industrious and courageous. There in France this young Chinese intellectual began to be proud of these countrymen of his, whom he had never known before. He began to feel a stir in his soul. These men, he told himself, were worth teaching.

He began to teach them and he found them both intelligent and eager. They wanted to learn. The more he taught them the more convinced he became that it was a deep injustice that they were illiterate and that to teach the common people of China was what he wanted to do above all else.

But how could this be done? The Chinese written language is complex and difficult. Scholars spend a lifetime perfecting their use of it. To recognize five thousand separate characters is a minimum even for ordinary reading. These five thousand characters, he decided, must be reduced to a much smaller number.

There in France he worked out a simplification of the Chinese language that was to be the basis for the whole scheme of mass education that followed. It was in effect a sort of basic Chinese. He put down to the best of his ability the one thousand characters for the words most used by the men, then he taught these characters to them. But when he had taught them, what had they to read? He found that he must supply their reading material. This he did by starting a little newspaper, so that immediately after they had learned their thousand characters, they had something on which they could use them. The whole venture was a great success.

Yet the important thing actually was not that a few thousand Chinese laborers were taught to read. The important thing was what happened to the young scholar. He was deeply shaken by the joy of these men. He saw that they had been suffering under a sense of their own ignorance. They had felt themselves blind because they could not read and write. When he saw them able to read even a little, when he saw what this meant to them, his own conversion was complete.

Of that conversion he told me later:

"I started the Chinese Laborer's Weekly in Paris, so that the men could read the news. They had been working blindly, knowing nothing even of the war in which they were workers. One day I received a letter from one of the men who had learned to read. It went something like this:

" 'Mr. Yen, big teacher: Ever since the publishing of your paper I began to know everything under the heavens. But your paper is so cheap and costs only one centime a copy, you may have to close down your paper soon. Here please find enclosed 365 francs which I have saved during my three years labor in France.'

"That is the kind of thing that touched me. I determined to use my life to enlarge his life. The word

'coolie' became for me a new word. I said, I will free
him from his bitterness and help him to develop his
strength."

From that day on James Yen never faltered in what
he wanted to do. He made up his mind to go back to
China and devote all that he was and all that he had
to the plain people of his own country.

A PEOPLE'S MOVEMENT

During my own years in China I heard of him now
and then. I did not live in the same part of China
where he was working. He began in Peking, and then,
inexplicably, or so I thought, he moved to a little district called Tinghsien, in Hopeh Province. There in
Tinghsien, I heard, he was conducting a sort of educational experiment. No one took it very seriously at
the time. How could you, when there were so many
millions of illiterate people in China? What was one
young man in one little district? The cynical said,
"What will his life count, and what will one little
district matter?"

But we kept hearing about him. He made marks
here and there on China or rather his idea did. One
never heard very much about him personally. It was
always the thing he was doing that was talked about.
He was trying to work out a system whereby in a
generation the people of China could be taught to
read and write. His thousand-character method began

to be known and other people tried it and found it worked very well, if they used the thousand-character literature that went with it.

Then one began to hear that it was not just a literacy movement. My own brother, who was a vital statistician and interested in public health, went to visit Tinghsien and came back saying that the movement was really a people's movement, and that public health was being carried on, too. Then it seemed something was being done in people's government. I began to be deeply curious about this little spot in China called Tinghsien. A ferment was there. Without publicity and without noise, it was working. But why only in one place? I made up my mind that year that when the weather grew cooler I would go and find out for myself.

Then the Japanese attacked China, and one thing and another happened, and I went to America instead. The war began in good earnest, and whatever was going on in Tinghsien had to go on under Japanese occupation. I even forgot about the whole thing, until I heard of the *hsien* (county) governments set up in Hunan. I connected this with the magnificent resistance of the Hunan people to the Japanese. In Hunan the Japanese have met their most bitter opposition. When I inquired I recognized something familiar in this new hsien government—it was the sort of people's government that had been set up in Tinghsien.

Then I heard that James Yen was coming to America. It was not the first time. He had come to America more than once for his people's education movement. But I scarcely knew him then, except as the driving fire of energy behind a seemingly impossible idea. I had met him and did not remember him, except as an energy which I had not understood.

Now after twenty years, here he was again in America and we met face to face. Both of us had changed but both of us somehow knew each other, because we had discovered without meeting that we were now ready to become friends and co-workers. We had come by different ways to the same conclusion, that the common man of any country is the important man and that there will be no peace nor joy in this world until his lot is made what he deserves. In both of us was a deep respect for this common man, and a deep determination to devote ourselves to his cause.

James Yen's spare frame was just as upright as ever, and it seemed to me that the fire that burned in him was even more clear and strong. He was still the single flame. His work had been his life, and now everything else was burned out of him. His kind abstract smile, his grave courtesy, will make him listen to you, but he is only biding his time until he can bring up his dominant interest, the education of the people.

But this interest is now as vast as the world. It grew in China to take in the whole life of the common man, not only his mind, but his body, not only his body but his house and his neighborhood, and his nation. To-day James Yen is thinking beyond the plain people even of China. He is thinking of the plain people everywhere.

We began to talk and we have never stopped talking. I wanted to get to the soul of this man and see what made it burn. One does not often, in this day or any day, find a man whose whole life has been completely selfless. James Yen is not so much better than other men, not so much more intelligent or able, that this can be explained only through his natural gifts. He has great natural gifts, but others have had as great who have done much less.

I found in him a deep and simple humility. There was even a sort of contriteness in him, an apology for his scholar-ancestors and for those of his country who have not known what the plain people of China are and so have not given them all through the centuries what they deserved and could have used. He is scorching in his condemnation of the intellectuals, old and new, who still hold themselves aloof from the people.

"I was one of them," he said frankly, when we first began to talk. "I myself didn't know our own people until I was in France, thrown into their midst there because of my five thousand coolies and men of labor. For the first time I began to see something of the bitterness and the distress of the people."

This man was something new to me. I had long been bitter enough myself about the intellectuals of China and my own books had been written on behalf of the people they too often despised. Here was an awakened intellectual. I wanted to know all about the awakening and what it had accomplished. But it was impossible to talk long enough hours in New York where we met. In a city time is telescoped and shot to bits. A day is a mass of fragments.

"Come home with us," I said to James Yen. "In the country time is like a great empty bowl. You can fill it with whatever you like. I want hours in which to ask you questions."

So he came, and after a night's rest we sat down in the Sunday silence of a summer morning, in the quiet library whose big window overlooks lake and woods, and we began to talk.

THE "WORLD'S FOUNDATION"

I only asked questions. It is his answers that are important. For as this Chinese sat there talking so earnestly, hour after hour, I saw unfolding not only the thing he had already done in China, but a plan, a tool, a technique, ready to be used anywhere in the world. I would have been interested enough had it been something only for China, for in China are one-fifth of the world's people. But it was something for far more than China.

"I feel this way about them," James Yen told me. "Our ancients said, 'People are the foundation of the nation. If the foundation is firm, then the nation will enjoy tranquillity.' I apply that to the whole world. People are the foundation of the world. If the foundation is firm then the world will enjoy tranquillity. But threee-fourths of the world's people today are underhoused, underclothed, underfed, illiterate. In other words, three-fourths of the world's foundation is rotten. Now as long as this continues to be true we have a very poor foundation upon which to build the world."

Outside the window the churchbells were ringing. I knew what the scene would be in our Pennsylvania village a mile away. The farmers and their wives and children would be walking together into the little Lutheran brick church, an old church where their forefathers had worshipped, too. I know these farmers somewhat, as I had known the farmers in China who are so like them. James Yen was really talking about the same people.

"I have visited many other countries," he was saying earnestly, "and I am convinced that the basic needs of man are the same. It is only when we get away from basic levels, which are universal, that things become complicated. Any people in any part of the world are entitled to a minimum of education, a minimum of livelihood, a minimum of health and self-rule. Now I feel that the basic principles and methods that have been developed in one part of the world for solving those basic problems of illiteracy, poverty, disease and misgovernment could be applied to other parts of the world which have the same problems, with, of course, the necessary but actually slight modifications and adaptations to local conditions. This program which we have been working out in China is the program that is needed now for the three-fourths of the world's people, because it is a program for reconstruction which can be carried out by the people themselves. They will become educated as they reconstruct their own lives. It is education through reconstruction, and reconstruction through education."

There was a power in these words. Here in America experts in education have been fumbling about for a generation with the idea of educating through doing. I had seen little shops in schools where the children tinkered at toys and models of real things. A few days ago I had heard a man who is held as a great exponent of adult education sigh and say sadly, "The adult education movement is dead. I don't know how to put life into it." Yet here was a Chinese literally flaming with confidence as he said, "They will be educated as they reconstruct their own lives." He spoke out of twenty-five years' experience. And people in other countries were hungry to meet him, to know what he was doing and how he was doing it. He had just had an invitation to come to Mexico and tell the Mexicans about the idea of education through reconstruction of life. He had just come back from Cuba.

A VISIT TO CUBA

"Tell me about your visit in Cuba," I said.

He smiled his half-sad smile. "I found it so much like China. Havana is beautiful—clean, modern, with a good public health service. Then the minute you step into the rural districts you see preventable diseases all around you everywhere. The people in the country are poor. Cuba must evolve a health system so inexpensive that the people can afford it, so simple that people can learn it themselves. Now that challenges the best minds in the whole field of public health there. But I use public health only as an example. The same thing applies to education, argriculture, economics, and government."

I recognized the four points of his plan for the people of China.

"I found the same thing in Cuba that I found in China—and in every other country," he went on. "Those who have learning keep it for themselves, to improve their own positions in life. They do not think of it as something which ought to be shared with all."

Someone in the house turned on a radio and a blare of war news burst into the room, through the half-opened door. We listened for a moment to the story

25

of bombs falling upon German towns, to the advances of Japanese armies. I rose and shut the door.

"Now is the time to begin this education through reconstruction everywhere in the world," James Yen said. "While the war is on, while the fight for freedom is still not won, people are thinking a little more than usual of the inter-relation of nations. I am afraid the moment the war is over and the pressure and tension are removed, they will fall back again into their old grooves and think the same way and do everything the same way, each for himself and his own nation only, and in another twenty years we will commit again the same crime against humanity. Yet we must not think of nations as units—we must think really internationally of peoples. The world is the unit—any other planning is futile. Educating one people is so useless unless all are educated for a better life. Even the movement for education through reconstruction in China can only be successful if the same thing is being done in other countries—there must be cooperation and collaboration throughout the world if the three-fourths of the world's people are to be brought up to their proper level. It is absolutely my conviction that after this war no movement that is of any significance in one nation can be carried out successfully and effectively without having it linked to a similar movement in every other country, so that all peoples are marching along together.

"That was really the reason I went to Cuba, just to test out this idea. When I got there I was asked to speak about some of the fundamental problems China is facing, illiteracy, poverty, disease, misgovernment, and how we were tackling these problems through a coordinated system of people's education, people's livelihood, people's health and people's government. My Cuban friends came to me afterwards and said: 'Mr. Yen, you were not talking about the problems of China—you were talking about the problems of Cuba. Here we have illiteracy, here we have poverty, here we have disease, here we have misgovernment.

" 'Isn't it interesting that our situation here is much like yours in China? Our intellectuals are very academic too. They live in ivory towers. Here you see this beautiful city of Havana and yet in the vast rural areas you see thousands and thousands of poor and ignorant people. We want this thing you have—it's something grown out of the people. We are going to stop talking, stop theorizing. We are going to do something, get an experiment started like your Tinghsien—a "Cuban Tinghsien." '

"It was really a great inspiration to me to see seven of the most outstanding citizens of Cuba organize themselves into a Board for mass education and social reconstruction for Cuba. These men, among them a noted professor, a prominent publisher, a business leader, a former Minister of Public Health, went to the rural districts to investigate, and I went with them, in order to pick out a typical community for the experiment. Finally, they selected what is called in Spanish a *municipio*, in Guanajay, in the province of Pinar del Rio, as their first experimental center. I don't know yet how they are getting along—politics or other factors might obstruct the work. But anyway, if there is anything of importance that could be done for Cuba, those seven fine men could certainly do it."

ONE FAMILY UNDER HEAVEN

He was on his feet again, pacing the floor as he does when he thinks deeply. "You see the principle of demonstration centers holds for each country. It's more scientific, more economical to do things thoroughly in one place first and then extend them. This in the long run is more time-saving. When we first went to Tinghsien, it was a mud and dust village. Who cared for that place? We stuck to that first human laboratory—for six years. Once the pattern was worked out, we knew other districts and provinces could take it up with great rapidity.

"If it can be done in China, it can be done anywhere in the world. As you educate the submerged three-fourths in literacy, livelihood, health and government while you teach them their first letters and their first principles, it is important to make them realize that there can be cooperation and happiness everywhere. As we have it in Chinese 'Under heaven, there is but one family.' When you get that world-sense into people they will think of themselves not as isolated units but as parts of a whole. Those people in the little town of Tinghsien—they had never thought of anyone except themselves. But now they know they are a part of the world. Do you know, they are carrying on their schools, their public health work and improved agriculture in spite of Japanese occupation? And even their local government is holding together."

He looked at me proudly. And I saw that little village, for I had seen thousands like it in the plains of northern China. It was a huddle of tiled roofs over mud-walled houses, a few wide dusty streets, surrounded by a low mud wall. The people were brown with dust and wind and sun, not often washed because the wells are shallow and few. Tinghsien is not different from all the others.

"How did you happen to choose that one town?" I asked with real curiosity.

My Pennsylvania housekeeper, trained in a few essential Chinese ways, came in with a pot of Chinese tea and some tea bowls. We had talked so long that we were properly grateful. James Yen sipped his tea before he answered.

"I'd like to hear the whole story of Tinghsien," I went on. "Make a demonstration of me, please. How are you going to tell everybody about it?"

He laughed. "Oh, it's a long story," he said. "But if you want it—"

He put down his tea bowl. "It was really rather haphazard. I went back to China from France with two or three friends like myself, all eager to work for our people. For the first three or four years we were thinking mostly of teaching the people just how to read and write. Well, where were the people? Certainly they were not in the beautiful city of Peking —a handful of them are there, of course, but not the millions and millions of them. They are scattered all over China in thousands of humble dusty hamlets and villages. 'All right,' we said to ourselves, 'we must go to them there.' "

"How did you start?" I asked.

I could see the people so clearly as I had seen them through many years in China, those brown hearty good country people, living out their lives as their ancestors had done before them and never seeing so much as the inside of a schoolhouse or even dreaming of such a thing as knowing how to read and write.

GOING TO THE PEOPLE

"It was several years before we got to Tinghsien. The city or county seat was the obvious place to start," he said. "We knew the great value of an 'educational atmosphere.' Any people who are illiterate and isolated are antagonistic towards anything new.

You talk about a railroad, they object to it. Public health? They don't understand it. But if you talk about *tu-shu* (reading books), they understand that. I suppose this is due to our centuries of traditions which have cultivated even in the illiterate a kind of reverence for learning. They appreciate *tu-shu* but they never dreamed that they could do it too. For centuries it has been beyond the farmer. But if you can go to the people and actually show them that they can *tu-shu*, then half the battle is won. Also the 'educational atmosphere' is necessary to get the conservative element in the community, which is the most influential, to allow the young people to study. The young people may be ever so eager, but if the heads of their families do not approve, that would be the end of it—especially for the girls.

"It required weeks of 'social calls' and group meetings to set the atmosphere. Then the campaign went on almost of itself. A big meeting of the townspeople elected a council to take charge of it. Schools were drawn in, and students volunteered to serve on recruiting teams. Events led up to a mass meeting and parade all around the town, to the gaping astonishment of the villagers who had come in to town for market day. There was hardly anyone left unaware of the literacy campaign, what it meant, what it stood for. The recruiting teams went from house to house, and there was no peace for a family until every illiterate between twelve and twenty-five had signed up.

"Wu-han [general name for the three cities: Wu-chang, Hankow, Henyang] was one of the most successful of our campaigns, and because of its central location and its historic setting it stirred the whole nation."

I remembered that it was at Wu-han the Chinese Revolution met with its final success and the Republic of China was established.

"At Wu-han, the enrollment of illiterate men and women, girls and boys, went far beyond our expectations. Over 20,000 enrolled, and this created a threatening problem of shortage of teachers. Urgent invitations were sent to the professors and students of the colleges, to principals and teachers of the middle schools and primary schools, for a big mass meeting held at the Central China University at Wuchang. We sent out altogether a thousand invitations. We thought that we would be fortunate if we could get five hundred of these teachers and students to come.

"When the time came, the auditorium of the University was crowded to overflowing. More than 1200 teachers and college students came. It was a great inspiration to me to see all those keen expectant faces. I spoke for two hours on the importance of the educated members assuming the responsibility of educating the uneducated. In conclusion I made this appeal to the audience, 'Those of you who are willing to volunteer to teach one hour a day without pay, please stand up.' Those 1200 men and women rose like one man and offered their services.

"But after a campaign like that you have to set up an organization, or it will fizzle out. So at Wu-han we formed a Mass Education Association, and in a quieter way the campaign spread to the villages. Demonstration schools were established in several centers with 'student teachers,' young men selected from the district, and given brief training. In addition to teaching at least two classes in his own school, each teacher had to get at least ten self-supporting People's Schools started in the neighboring villages."

"And how was the work done in the villages?"

HOW IT'S DONE

He smiled. "I'll tell you how we do it now, after all that we learned in those days. The first thing we do is call on the Village Elder. He is like the head of the family. Usually he is known for his fine character, or his philanthropy, or his scholarship. If he doesn't know anything or doesn't have much, he is simply a good honest man with gray hair and a long beard, whom everybody respects and loves.

"You call on him and ask him how many people in the village read. He says I don't know. What about finding out? He doesn't care. If we are going to have this village rich and strong it would be a good thing to have it educated. He says that's impossible. So we begin to tell him about what we have actually accomplished in a big city. (In the city we told the people what we had done in France!) I say, how about trying it in your own village, and have the honor of being the first village to have education? We know the technique. We know how to teach. But you must come out and tell the people what to do. If we tell them they won't believe it.

"Then he says, I have a few associates on the Village Council and we must go and call on them. We say fine, but you must do the talking. You must tell them we have already taught the people. You tell them what we have done. (We used to have moving pictures of every stage in the campaigns, but now they are all in the hands of the Japanese or destroyed.) So we'd call on the members of the Council, his associates. We would sip and sip tea and talk. Pretty soon we would find someone who was related to someone in our group, or a friend of a friend. Immediately, you are friends and equals—or even relatives! Then they want you to stay for dinner and they serve you rice wine. Maybe not much but there is friendliness, joviality. So they are very happy.

"Then we say, how about calling a meeting tomorrow? They say fine. We say, get all the families to come out. Fine! But where? In the temple. Every village, no matter how big or small, how rich or how poor, has a temple with an open air theatre. These temples also serve as social community centers for these country people. They say, it will be done. They will call a meeting tomorrow and will get all the heads out.

"The people couldn't read or write so they couldn't put up a notice about a meeting. A man would go around to each section of the village, a sort of town crier, beating a gong. Everybody would come out and he would announce: Tomorrow at the temple theatre there will be a very important meeting. Everybody must be there. Scholars from the city have come to this village.

"Everybody is excited. Who would come to our village? So they all come to the meeting to find out. They all go on talking until the gong sounds again and everybody grows quiet. The Village Elders are there. The little old ladies, their children and grandchildren, even the dogs! Everybody comes to see us, just as though we were a circus.

"Then the village elder starts to speak. 'I called you together for a very important meeting. It concerns the prestige of this village. These gentlemen are self-sacrificing scholars. They have come to our miserable, despicable village to educate us, to make scholars of us.' I would get up and talk but I wasn't too good. Then the Elder would call on one of the men who could speak their jargon—not really a dialect but more like a drawl, like American speech of the deep South. It was important to get one of the local people to talk.

"He says, 'Do you have eyes? Everybody here who has eyes, raise his hand.' They all raise their hands. 'Can you see me?' They all answer yes. 'Here's a book. How many of you can see this?' Everybody raises his hand again. 'How many of you can read this?' Nobody answers. 'You have eyes, that's true, but you can't read. You are just as bad as blind. We have doctors here who can cure this disease. They have studied in Chinese schools and in western schools. They have come to cure your disease. They are very patient. They will keep on treating you until you are cured. If you were really blind, how long would it take to cure you? But these scholars know how to cure your disease in four months! You don't need to pay any money. You only spend one hour a day. In four months your blindness will be cured.'

"By this time they are all laughing and smiling. They enjoy the talk but don't believe it. Then he says, 'Those who are willing to come to school, hands up!' One would very timidly put up his hand and then pull it down again. Then the Village Elder gets impatient. He says, 'Now look here, Lao Wang, you don't know how to read. You put your hand up. Come on, hands up.' And Lao Wang sheepishly puts up his hand again. Then, perhaps a little twelve year old boy raises his hand. In a little while everybody has

36

put up his hand—three or four hundred, depending on the size of the village, and on the Village Elder. If he is good he can get the whole village to sign up. We do not want too many pupils to begin with.

"So the enrolling is finished that way and perhaps we have thirty or forty for our first class. The Village Elder or one of the rich members perhaps will give us one or two rooms, or sometimes we use the temple. The teacher is one of our trained men. He knows the technique of teaching these people and knows how to draw them out. He starts out with the people who have enrolled in the class but they go back home and talk to their families about it. So when the class goes on you have people peeking in through the windows.

"While we have one of our trained men start the class, we find out who are the literate members, if any, in the village and train them to be teachers. Then, the second week, perhaps, the village teachers will take over the school. That is the typical beginning of a People's School."

A SCHOOL FOR EVERY VILLAGE

"The first school was really experimental. After we learned the 'what' and the 'how' we would start three or four demonstration schools in centrally located villages. To these the teachers of the old-fashioned schools and other literate members of the community were invited. Once they saw how practical

37

the teaching material was and how simple the teaching method, they would start classes of their own and teach the illiterates in their respective communities without pay. These schools, taught and supported by the people themselves are the 'People's Schools.' The responsibility of staffing and financing the experimental schools and the demonstration schools is ours. But the responsibility of staffing and financing the 'People's Schools' falls upon the people. In Tinghsien, we conducted only two experimental schools and six demonstration schools for the whole district. But the people of Tinghsien ran 472 'People's Schools,' that is, one for every village, all supported by themselves.

"We soon began to see that when the minds of the people were liberated, they wanted more and they needed more. We realized that literacy alone was not enough. Literacy isn't education—it is only a tool for education, a means to the whole end. The people had to get an education which involved the whole of their life. And life in China for them is very unsatisfactory. So their education, if it is of the right kind, should be not so much to fit them *for* life as to *re-make* life. Later you will see how we tackled public health, agriculture, economics and local government."

MADAME HSIUNG

James Yen suddenly broke off to smile. "Now is the time to tell you about Madame Hsiung. She had bound feet and belonged to the old, old school. Her father had been an official in Hunan. She had studied the classics when she was a girl, and was able to compose essays and poems, and she was skilled in Chinese calligraphy, too. Her father had married her to a Han-lin scholar who became later the Premier of the Republic. But all those years while her husband was in the Cabinet, people said it was really Madame Hsiung who was the brains, the 'man behind the gun.'

"One day when we had our experiments going, I said: 'It's high time I invited Madame Hsiung to come and see what we are doing.' I invited her to come to a Commencement we were having in Shantung, home province of Confucius—that was back in August, 1923, long before we ever went to Tinghsien. Madame Hsiung was then about 50 years old. I asked her to come and make the Commencement speech and distribute the diplomas.

"Well, she made the Commencement speech, and she saw all those who had learned to read, 1500 of them, old men, old women, young men, young women, little children, ranging all the way from eight years of age to fifty-six. I wish you could have heard Madame Hsiung's speech.

"She looked out over the hall and she said, 'Here

is something I have never seen in my life before. You have old men and young men and women. I see a boy over there bare-footed, that little girl there with an apron.' She went on, 'This is real education for a free and equal people. This is the only way to realize a people's government. This is education and democracy. This is education for democracy.' She was so moved by what she saw, all those people, holding their diplomas, able at last to read and write! (Then she broke down and wept.)

"Then she said, 'I am President of the Women's League and am President of the National Women's Red Cross. I am going to resign from them all now and give my life to this people's education.'

"From that day, August 1, 1923, she gave up everything else. Being a Chinese woman of the old school and of a conservative official family she was confined a great deal to the home. She had bound feet, yet after she caught the vision of educating China's masses, she was so inspired and became so self-sacrificing that she hardly ever stayed in her comfortable home in Peking, but traveled incessantly from province to province to promote education for the people. You should have seen her talk to the intellectuals in Peking, in Shanghai. She went to the head of the government at Nanking, Marshal Chi Hsieh-yuan, and got him so interested that he gave $10,000 to the campaign and established the first city Mass Education Association, in Nanking.

"We were doing quite a lot. For example, we used to work in the armies of the big warlords. We felt there was no hope for China if the civil wars went on. But before we could eliminate militarism we felt we had to educate the soldiers, so that was why we went into the armies. We were welcomed everywhere by the warlords as 'revered teachers.' You know that in our country they have great respect for the teacher. We accepted no money from any of the warlords, and we even paid our own traveling expenses in order to show that we had no ulterior motives. We went wherever we were asked and whenever our specific jobs of planning and training were over we came away again. In this way we scattered the seeds of mass education."

He smiled again. "I must tell you how Madame Hsiung tackled the big Marshal Hsiao Yui-lan. That was in 1924. He was in Hankow and he was unfortunately already smoking opium by then. She and I went to call on him. We waited three hours before he came out to see us. We knew that he was smoking and could not come until he had finished. When he finally appeared this was the gist of what she said to him—I remember it all so well. 'Marshal, our country is going to pieces and falling into ruin. You know why. The reason is that on one hand we have these millions of uneducated people, and on the other, these leaders, dishonest and even themselves uneducated.

Why, some of them are actually opium smokers! What hope is there for China?'

"Then she said, 'Marshal, we must do something and you must help us. Really you ought to help us educate the nation. We are all bound together, the people are the foundation of the nation. If the foundation is solid, the nation will enjoy tranquillity. Will you help us in this work?'

"I was so embarrassed by her directness—but he gave us $10,000! Well, that was the kind of thing she did. She got the leading men in the provinces to call in her name a National Congress on Mass Education in Peking and we had over five hundred delegates representing the government and people's institutions from twenty-one provinces and special districts. Those were memorable days!"

NATIONAL ASSOCIATION OF THE MASS EDUCATION MOVEMENT

"Our national association was organized out of that National Congress, and Madame Hsiung was elected chairman. This was another remarkable thing. We had nine members on our Board of Trustees, three Cabinet members and some of the most prominent men representing education, business, and industry. You should have seen Madame Hsiung preside over that group of dignitaries. They all respected her and did practically everything she wanted them to do.

"It was she who supported the Movement at the beginning. We started in the fall of 1924. The first year, of course, we had very little money—only $3600. That included my salary and that of a part-time clerk and a part-time servant. We had city associations like Nanking, Hankow, and Canton, and out of the $3600 we paid for everything. The next year our expenses were $6000 and Madame Hsiung paid them out of her own pocket. She wasn't rich but just well-to-do.

"Oh, she was a wonderful woman! When she stood up to speak to groups of intellectuals and business men she would speak two or three hours at a time, and she had such small feet that she could not stand steadily, so she had to move about continually, and all the people, even through those many hours, would listen attentively. You know, here is an extraordinary thing about our country that Westerners do not understand. Women in our country are supposed to have an inferior position as compared to men, but whenever a woman attains power in the home or in scholarship, whenever a woman really has vision and a personality, she is regarded even more highly than a man with the same qualifications. The fact that she is a woman and yet that she has such an education, such a vision, makes her all the more respected, admired and exalted.

"So Madame Hsiung worked and toiled for nearly eight years. Then she died. She was known throughout China in those years between 1923 and 1930. We even had an overseas division then—did you know that?"

I did not and said so. In those days I was living in a small walled town in North China myself and nobody came in and nobody went out. What was happening outside of our town meant little to me then.

HELP FROM OVERSEAS CHINESE

James Yen went on. "It was in Honolulu, and it came about almost accidentally. I'll tell you about it— just to show how this idea catches fire among the people. In 1935 I went to Honolulu to represent China at an Institute of Pacific Relations conference. I was one of twelve delegates. At the close of the conference I was the last speaker. I spoke about our work, and had an unusual response. The whole audience rose as one man and clapped. The Chairman, Dr. Ray Lyman Wilbur, said, 'We have met here for two weeks and we have discussed sixty different topics. We have heard a lot of speeches. But the one thing that is going to have more to do with the future of peace of the nations bordering on the Pacific than any other is this mass education movement in China. What direction these hundreds of millions of illiterate people of China will take, how they will develop and what philosophies they are going to be educated in will have more to do with the future of the Pacific than any other one thing.'

"Well, the papers published all this the next morning and the Chinese were excited and they approached me and said, 'Now, Mr. Yen, you must stay and tell us what you have been telling the Institute people,' and that was how I happened to stay for two more weeks after the conference. During those weeks I made some thirty speeches to large and small groups.

"One of the results of those meetings was that an intense interest was aroused in Chinese language study, especially among the energetic Chinese young men and young women born in Honolulu. Many of them had already had high school education, and quite a few even college education, but they did not have an additional opportunity of studying the Chinese language. It happened that an old friend and Yale classmate of mine, Professor S. C. Lee, was then teaching Chinese history and literature at the University of Hawaii. Lee and an American instructor of Chinese got together and organized a special school for teaching the 'People's Thousand Character Readers.' Their first class graduated 104 students including three Koreans.

"Those Chinese compatriots of ours would crowd the auditorium two and three thousand at a time. At one of those big meetings at the Chinese Chamber of

Commerce a man got up and said, 'Now that we can do something for our fatherland, we must do something.' Another man got up and said, 'We cannot go back to China to join Mr. Yen but we can certainly give money to this movement to educate our people.' You know, in all the years, I had never appealed for money in my public addresses. I would just talk about why we did it, how we did it and what it meant to our country and to the world. Still another man got up and said, 'Yes, let's organize and raise money.'

"So those men got together and organized teams to raise money among the Chinese of Honolulu. They had over 300 different members organized into twelve different teams. They had a ladies' team, dentists' team, doctors' team, girls' team, boys' team, bankers' team and all kinds. They canvassed from house to house, every Chinese in the island, to give something. Oh, it was an extraordinary experience!

"And one afternoon I was told to go and call on Chinese people who were well-to-do, and a banker went with me to see a man named Chuk, a grocery store keeper. 'I heard you speak,' this man said to me. 'China needs just what you are trying to do. We are all blind, you know.' Then he went on talking. 'I'm blind, too—I can't read. I have the bitterness of being blind. I would like to help this movement, so you can get our fellow countrymen to read and open their eyes. I'm a poor man, but I have saved some money.

I would like to give you the one thousand dollars which I have saved.'

"I was so touched! He was just like a 'coolie,' that is, a toiler, and he talked like a 'coolie,' but it was just that sort of man that made me go on with the work. When men like that talk to me and when they appreciate the little we do, when they pour out their hearts as well as their money—that is what drives me on and makes me forget myself."

He paused, forgetting himself, indeed, and everything else, except the man whom he remembered and the millions like him in China. You cannot be with James Yen for five minutes without knowing that long ago he forgot himself forever.

"In three days' time," he went on, "those Chinese under the leadership of a banker, Charles Wang, a dentist, Dr. Chang, and Professor Lee had raised over $20,000 in Honolulu and there were only 20,000 Chinese in the whole island. When Governor Farrington entertained me at tea, he gave me the grip—we belonged to the same college fraternity—and he said, 'Brother Yen, I congratulate you. During all the time I have been in Honolulu the Chinese have proved themselves our most law-abiding citizens. Now in three days they have raised all this money without any preparation. I am more than ever proud of them.'"

AMERICAN FRIENDS

"When I revisited this country 16 years ago at the invitation of my Alma Mater, Yale, a great many friends offered to give a hand. It is impossible to mention their names individually, but Mr. Gerard Swope gave most valuable aid in making important contacts, and the real genius, Mr. Edward C. Carter, of the Institute of Pacific Relations, gave practically all of his time to the work. He put his whole heart and soul into it. Under his able chairmanship a group of very distinguished Americans representing education and industry was organized.

"Another friend who freely gave his full time and energy to the work was Frederick V. Field, who had just graduated from Harvard. Fred gave up a trip to Europe in order to serve voluntarily as my secretary and for the next nine months he traveled with me from one end of the United States to the other.

"Among the women who came forward was Ellen Auchincloss (now Mrs. Gordon M. Tiffany), who joined the Movement in 1929 and for six years served it faithfully and efficiently in China as its English secretary. Miss Auchincloss, who belonged to a fine New York family, not only shared our ideals at Tinghsien but also lived as the rest of us did. She had her quarters in a mud house and wore the rough blue cotton clothing of the village people.

"The Milbank Memorial Fund helped us through

Mr. John Kingsbury and Mr. Edgar Sydenstricker who came to visit us himself. Through its China Program under the direction of its Vice-President, the late Mr. Selskar M. Gunn, a rare soul and a scientist of broad vision, the Rockefeller Foundation gave the Movement substantial support.

"During my stay in America I met some really world-minded and farseeing men and women. Their understanding of what we were trying to do and the backing they gave was a great inspiration to me and my colleagues. Really, for what has been achieved by the Movement so far an important share of the credit is due to farsighted and generous American friends."

I could see that this Chinese loves to muse over the wonderful and kind things that people have done for him. It does not seem to occur to him that they are done for him. He does not separate himself at all from his work. To him the work is so important that when people help him he thinks they are as deeply inspired as he is by the thought of the people. Yet I knew that James Yen, had he been more mindful of himself, could have been a great political leader in his own country had he chosen that path.

THE WARLORDS

So I asked, "You said that the old warlords invited you to help them?"

"Yes, nearly all of them did. Some invited us out

49

of conviction. Most of them, however, did so because they did not want to be left out. To invite the Mass Education Movement to conduct education or to start a training institute for officials began to be looked upon as a sign of being progressive. So, as we say in Chinese, 'We keep one eye shut and the other one open.' As long as we were doing some good we didn't want to be too particular about questioning people's motives!

"I'll tell you about one warlord. He was a friend of long standing because we had helped to educate his army. One day he wanted me to come for a long talk and sent his car for me. The gist of our conversation was this.

"He said: 'Yang-chu, my old friend, you have been working hard these years for the Mass Education Movement, but it would be a mistake for you to devote your whole life to it. Furthermore, you have always had great difficulty in getting enough funds, and you are always over-worked. I'm a great believer in mass education, and I want to do everything possible to back it up. But I do not believe that you should continue to carry on *yourself*. A man of your talents should get into politics and leave mass education to your colleagues, who I understand are men of high caliber and are perfectly capable of carrying on.

"My proposition is this, that in order to relieve you of having to raise money year in and year out, I will be glad to offer you an endowment of $8,000,000 for mass education. Delegate your responsibilities to your colleagues. Then you would be free to get into politics without which you won't be able to carry out the objectives of your Movement. If you consent to join and take the lead, I have no doubt that the best returned students and the most progressive elements will join us too. You know how important that is in the service of our country.'

"We talked back and forth. I was closeted with him for over four hours and was showered with questions and arguments. Finally, I said to him: 'In all important matters I always consult my colleagues. Let me talk the whole thing over with them.'

"The session I had with my senior colleagues of the Movement lasted from nine in the evening to four in the morning. What made us deliberate so long was not whether we should accept the $8,000,000 endowment or whether I should agree to enter politics, but how we could decline both offers tactfully and gracefully without offending a very powerful warlord!

"My answer to him the next day was in brief this—'We have been friends for so many years that we ought to be able to be perfectly frank with each other, and furthermore, our one common interest is in the uplift of China. I feel one of the great mistakes that our leaders have made in the past is that they have paid little or no attention to the foundation work of the country. My own conviction is that unless we

51

have a strong foundation, we can never have a strong China and that foundation is the people, the masses. I feel I ought to stick to the people and build the foundation, and that you ought to stick to political and military affairs as you have a unique opportunity. You work for China from the top down, I'll work from the bottom up.

"We are both young yet, and can both have the time and energy to give to China our best. Ten years from now, if we both make good, each in our own line, then we must join together in a common program for the reconstruction of China. When that time comes we shall not only have able leaders, mature and experienced, but also followers, millions of them, intelligent and enlightened.' My old friend appeared impressed if not convinced.

"Of course, my colleagues and I realized that political power is important but we also realized that developing the power of the people is even more fundamental—if we aim to build a democracy in China. At the time when that offer was made there were flood and famine as well as civil war in China. The Movement had to struggle for its existence. But my colleagues and I were absolutely one in this, 'What does it profit a man if he should gain the whole world and lose his own soul?' So with the Movement."

He took up his tea bowl again. I had another question to ask. "Haven't I heard that you and your colleagues were once in prison? Did your refusal of the warlord's offer have something to do with it?"

"Yes," he said. "My colleagues were put in prison. One day in the early spring of 1928 some two hundred soldiers armed with pistols surrounded our national headquarters in Peking. A dozen or so of them entered the office and demanded, 'Where's your General Director, Yen Yang-chu?'

"I happened to be absent in Tientsin at the time. Chen Chu-san was acting in my place. Chen was a college president before he joined us. Before that he was a senator in the first Parliament, and was active in fighting against Yuan Shih-kai's monarchical scheme and had barely escaped assassination. Being an old revolutionary and accustomed to being arrested, he stepped forward and asked the men, 'What do you want?' 'Your General Director,' they said. Chen replied, 'He's not here just now, but I'm acting in his place. What do you want?' 'We want to arrest him!' they exploded. 'He isn't here, I told you, so you'll have to arrest me.' Not only Chen was arrested that day and put in prison but all our colleagues who were working in the office at the time.

"When I returned from Tientsin, I was warned at the railroad station not to return home or go to the office as both places were surrounded and watched. I decided to go to the central office of the Chief of the Gendarmerie, where my colleagues were imprisoned. I demanded an explanation from the General.

53

But all he could say was that he had acted upon orders from above. Then I asked to be put in prison and have my colleagues set free. But he wouldn't do it. After two full days of negotiations and telegraphing the order came from 'above' to have our colleagues released.

"When I went to the cell to get my colleagues, I found the door open. I walked in and saw Chen Chu-san first. He was sitting with his back towards me and talking to the two prison guards. I called to him, but he did not hear me. Neither he nor the guards even noticed my entrance. I soon saw that he was 'preaching' the 'Thousand Characters' to those two illiterates! The guards had hoped that Mr. Chen, who had already become their friend, would teach them to read. Those two men were in tears when Mr. Chen parted with them!"

A SOCIAL LABORATORY—TINGHSIEN

"It was not long after that you all moved to Ting-hsien," I said. "You have not told me yet how you happened to go there."

"You know there are about 1900 hsien or counties in China and since the country is predominantly rural, the life pattern in one hsien is very similar to that of another. So we said, 'Why do we not just choose one hsien as our social or human laboratory? The chemist has a chemical laboratory, the physicist a physics laboratory, those of us who want to study human problems and solve them ought to have a human laboratory.' We had been going around to look for this laboratory.

"We were getting invitations from the gentry, who thought it would give their villages prestige to start a modern school. We had the most urgent invitation from one of the leading gentry in Tinghsien, a man by the name of Mi. He had gone to Japan to study and when he came home he was dissatisfied with his home town. He tried to reform everything at once. One of the things he did was to destroy the idols in the temples. Of course the people were furious and he could make no headway. You see, he didn't try to get the people to co-operate with him. He tried to do everything himself. And our country people are stubborn and independent. He was so disheartened he gave up the whole thing as hopeless. When he heard that we wanted to select a county for intensive study and work he said, 'I am a failure, but I will approach Mr. Yen and offer my village to him.' So he put the village at our disposal, and in it was only a little primary school he had started. I once taught such a school myself for a year."

PH.D'S BACK TO THE VILLAGE

"A colleague of mine, Dr. Fugh, a Chinese returned student and a Ph.D. in rural education, also went to that little mud village—the very first time a Chinese Ph.D. had ever lived and worked in such a village! His father was a scholar, like mine. We went to learn from the people.

"We didn't take our families at first. We lived in a little corner of the dilapidated temple and we made friends with the villagers.

"Other men joined us later. I must tell you about one, also a Ph.D. Fung was a specialist in agriculture and rural economics and had had fine training in agriculture and forestry in Cornell. Then he went to Rome and studied in the International Institute of Agriculture there. One day in Peking I bumped into him and I told him what we were trying to do in Tinghsien. I said, 'Would you like to join us?' He said, 'I will think it over.' A week afterwards he came to see me in my office at Peking and said, 'Mr. Yen, I have decided to join you. I've been back in China now for four years teaching agriculture in the university but as yet I don't even know a Chinese farmer. I want to get near our farmers—I want to know them.'

'So he resigned as head of the rural department in the university and came to Tinghsien. He was a dynamic fellow. He joined Dr. Fugh and they made a fine team in educational and agricultural work. Fugh started with two demonstration schools in that sub-county of sixty villages but later there were over sixty different People's Schools, all started by the people and run by the people themselves. Then Fung came along as the agriculturist to make experiments too, in his line. He had only 15 mou (one mou is equivalent to 1/6 of an acre) of land at first. He wanted to grow extra big cabbages but the first year he didn't do well. He had a hard time! His cabbages were no good and the farmers laughed at him."

We both laughed. I could see the young Ph.D. in the Chinese village and I could hear that hearty Chinese laughter. I had heard my farmer neighbors here in Pennsylvania laugh at a county agent that way, too.

"But Fung did better the next year," James Yen went on, "and the third year he did so well that the village people offered him 65 mou of land. Even Mr. Mi came back to see his village. He was so inspired to see what was happening that he called the rest of the gentry to meet together and they decided to let us have 1200 mou of their land for our experiments.

"One other reason why we went to Tinghsien was that there was a famous old civil service examination hall of Sung architecture. The gentry told us that if we would come to Tinghsien they would give us that hall for our headquarters. I could not resist it, and when Fugh's favorable report came to me, and Fung told me of his success in agriculture and that the people wanted us and showed us their sincerity by giving us land—well, we just had to accept. That meant we had to give up all the work we had been doing in the cities.

"And Tinghsien was also a typical place. The people in the county were poor but not too poor. They produced cotton, as do many such districts in North China. And we also liked the fact that there were 400,000 people in the county. That was a convenient, manageable unit for us to study, representing about one-thousandth of China's population.

"By 1929, there were about sixty of us in Tinghsien, including Chinese college graduates, quite a few professors, some officials, and two college presidents. One was the head of the National Law University and another was a great artist and head of the National Art College, both of Peking. They were creative men. That, by the way, was probably the first time in our country's history that the scholars and modern scientists had gone to the people."

He took a bit of paper from his pocket. "Here is what the leading Peking newspaper said at the time." He read, 'It was the most magnificent exodus of the intelligentsia into the country that had taken place in Chinese history to date. Holders of old imperial degrees, professors of national universities, a college president and former member of the National Assembly, and a number of Ph.D's and M.D's from leading American universities left their positions and comfortable homes in the cities to go to the backwoods of Tinghsien, to find out ways and means to revitalize the life of an ancient, backward people, and to build democracy from the bottom up.'

He laid down the paper, and went on. "There had been a great deal of outcry about 'back to the people' for years, but who ever went! Once in a while some-one who was kind-hearted or who wanted to be a reformer would go to a village to do something—like Mr. Mi, full of fervor and zeal, but he went as an individual, as a philanthropist. When they came up against opposition, which was natural, they would be-come discouraged, and finally give up. Scholars would write about the toil and struggle of the common peo-ple. Poets have glorified the simplicity and beauty of the life of the Chinese farmer. But all these tributes to the farmer did nothing to ease his burden.

"Even an internationally famous European intel-lectual wrote about the happiness of the Chinese farmer. He visited the rural parts of China. After a good chicken dinner and fine champagne, and with a pipe in his mouth, he was carried in a sedan chair by four coolies to see the country people. He came back and wrote, as our scholars did, about the tranquillity of the farmer. Or there might be a magistrate who was a fine leader. He would make some reforms and im-prove the lot of the people in his locality, but soon he would die or be promoted or demoted and the whole program would collapse again."

A DIFFERENT APPROACH

"Our approach was different. First of all, we must not ourselves be alien to the people. Chinese students who come to the United States would stick together and build a little 'Chinatown.' We had said to ourselves that we must not go to Tinghsien and build a 'little Peking.' We would go to a farmer and say: 'Do you have one or two spare rooms in your house?' If he said yes, we would tell him why we came. Most of the farmers couldn't understand, but they did appreciate the importance of education. We would go from farmer to farmer to find living quarters with them. An innovation we made in these houses was to provide windows. The farmhouse had no windows, only small holes for light and air, with paper pasted tightly over them. We would punch bigger holes for windows in the mud walls. One way you could tell where the mass education people lived was by looking for the walls with bigger holes.

"One dilemma we had as we went along was this: to learn the conditions and the attitudes of the village people and to identify ourselves with them was wholesome, but as the Chinese term reconstruction implies 'change and build,' what are the things we should change on the one hand and what are the things we should build on the other hand? How to strike a balance? We respect the traditions of the people, and one of the things we must always bear in mind is that *while we aim to create a new society, we must not forget we are doing it with an old society.*

"About one-third of our staff gave up and went back to Peking. Some who came with enthusiasm, eager to live and to work with the people, couldn't make any headway because they could not adapt themselves. Here was a man who had taught economics. We wanted him to study the books of the farmers, but he didn't know how or where to start. Trained men who had studied the finest textbooks in the biggest universities, and had taught hundreds of students, didn't know how to apply their knowledge to meet the needs of the farmers.

"Others left because they couldn't endure the country life. It was very dusty when it was dry, and when it was wet the mud was three or four inches deep. There were no cinemas, no theatres, no mah-jong parties. Some left because their wives couldn't stand it; some couldn't see the problems before them; still others saw the problems but didn't know what to do about them. It was nerve-wracking to solve problems. Certainly it was much easier and more comfortable to teach what some noted professor had taught and at the same time be looked upon as a great scholar!"

James Yen was on his feet again, standing and looking down at me with that intense and penetrating gaze of his.

"While you are searching for content or method you must have first-rate men, making first-rate plans and doing first-rate work. But the result of their experimental work ought to be such that a man with an indifferent educational background can use it and apply it. Therein lies the secret."

"The highly qualified men set the pattern and lead the way," I repeated.

"Also, it is they who must find the why and the how," James Yen replied. "That takes creative research. What is important is the result of their study. Their findings must be such that the average man can understand and appreciate them."

DYNAMIC RESEARCH

"When you say research," I told him, "I think of someone in a laboratory, or in a library full of books, in a university somewhere, far away from the people."

James Yen made one of his rare gestures of impatience.

"No, no," he exclaimed. "I mean dynamic research directly related to the life and needs of the people. Take a simple illustration. When my colleagues prepared texts they didn't just write them sitting in their armchairs. They went out and lived with the people to learn to know them—their long points, their short points and their basic needs. After they made the texts, they distributed them to the schools for trial. Based upon the criticisms of the teachers and of the students, the texts were revised and improved from season to season and year to year."

"So in Tinghsien," I said, "you started demonstration schools and you had the examination hall as your headquarters. But those Tinghsien people were farmers—they couldn't come to schools. When did they study?"

"Either early in the morning or late at night during the summer months," he replied. "But during the winter we had plenty of time. It was wonderful in the winter. Yet even in summer we taught them according to each pressing need as it came. For instance, when it was smallpox time we taught them about vaccination. Of course when we taught we didn't just talk. You can talk and talk about agriculture or health and they think, 'yes, that is fine,' but they don't quite believe in it for themselves. It is only when we demonstrated that education was possible for them that they wanted to take it up.

"Now those farmers were not stupid by any means. No, they were very intelligent. When you put an idea into their heads they were very keen to get education, to make a better living, to shape better things. In any part of this work, if you want to create a better order in any community, in any nation, you must first stimulate the minds of the people so that they demand the thing you have to give them. That is the beginning, and there is no success until then. A few experts or

63

officials going into a district is no use. As Confucius says, 'When the reformer lives, the reform lives, but when he dies, it dies with him.' Reform must take root in the people, it cannot be superimposed. That is why we started schools first—we wanted to open up the minds of the people."

He pressed his lips together for a moment and then began rather abruptly. "You know, there are some who call these illiterate people of China ignorant. They are not ignorant. They suffer from mental stagnation. Because they cannot read, their mental horizons do not go beyond their immediate neighborhood."

I had to interrupt him there. "But we have plenty of that mental stagnation right here in America. I should say that our people suffer from mental stagnation in spite of the fact that most of them can read if they want to, and that we listen to radio and see motion pictures. In China you say learning to read was a stimulant to the people. But how can you explain the fact that we Americans don't always see beyond our own horizon? Even when we can read?"

FELLOW SCHOLARS

James Yen's small brilliant eyes twinkled. "Yes, you have a sort of illiteracy, too. But it is easier than ours. You have at least the tool of literacy and that is the first step. But in China we had to give them even the tool. To be able to read—that opened up the mental life of the people. Well, you have a mind that is stimulated and then a desire is created in that mind. Sometimes you think only of your objective— the people are dirty, but they don't realize they are dirty. They are poor, but they are so used to it they scarcely know they are poor. You create a desire for better living. You give them a standard. And lastly, you create a community feeling. You see, in China we only have the feeling of the clan. Each family is clannish. Each is a unit. But when they had all been to school together they developed a sense of fellowship.

"You know those People's Schools had such a psychological effect on the farmers. For the first time the farmer could call himself a scholar. It was a position to which he had aspired for centuries but he had never been given a chance to reach it. Now that he could read he was really a scholar. That spells magic to a Chinese farmer. It created self-respect and self-confidence and dignity in him. And then the alumni began to have that fellow scholar feeling in the community. You can organize that for the community. And the women have it, too. There is your foundation for the reconstruction of the community. You have your nucleus in those men and women and there is your potent motivating force for the re-making of the whole community, or of the whole nation. Now that is a very, very important thing.

"But if you stop there? Then that would bring disaster. There begins the downfall of education. I say sometimes that non-education is better than mis-education. Now when these people want a better living and a better life, that is wholesome. But, if you only instill into them a lot of new ideas and new desires and don't equip them with real knowledge or real skills to satisfy their new desires then all you have done is to make a disturbance in the community of a very undesirable kind. People have come to me and said, 'Mr. Yen, you educate these farmers, maybe they will want to be white collar workers—and they won't want to farm any more.' 'Well,' I say, 'that is mis-education then.' When you have created a desire on the part of the people for better living, if you have caused a really divine discontent, which is so wholesome and fine, then you must immediately follow it with something practical.

"As we found out, we had to have the literacy program related definitely with a larger, broader program of life-betterment. You don't have to take the people away from their environment—from the farm— you educate them right there on the farm. You don't need to send them back to the farm, because you have never taken them away. So many well-meaning philanthropists take boys and girls away and put them into luxurious buildings and teach them and then wonder why they don't want to go back. We never did that. We taught them right where they lived. And after they had finished school they organized Fellow-Scholar Associations."

He looked at me with a half-smile. "I don't need to tell you not to laugh at our 'Fellow Scholars'."

I did not need to answer. Both of us saw those eager good faces, young and old. None could laugh at them for their content in having at last learned to read.

YOUTH GROUP—THE SPEARHEAD

"As far as reconstruction is concerned—and time is pressing—the old ones are too old and the little ones are too little. We must do this national reconstruction within this generation. For this reason the middle group, that is, the youth group, is most strategic. Ten years hence the young men and women now under twenty-five will be the leaders of the country, for good or for ill. There are sixty million unschooled Chinese, male and female, between twelve and twenty-five. In Tinghsien, while our educational program was open to all, we laid special emphasis upon the 80,000 young men and women, for if we could train these young people we would have developed a pattern for training the rest of the sixty million.

"So, after they are through with the People's Schools and have received their diplomas as 'Literate

67

Citizens' they organize themselves into what we call in Chinese *tung hsueh hwei*, meaning 'Fellow-Scholar Association.' It has a two-fold purpose. One is to continue to learn. The other purpose is to band together to reconstruct the community. These 'graduates' are the primary force for reconstructing the whole county. Visualize a 'Fellow-Scholar Association' scattered in the four hundred odd villages of the county. These men and women have had the same educational background and they're an organized force. They have a strong sense of fellowship and they feel a new sense of power. Each one of them must teach others, so they begin to organize little classes in their villages."

GUIDING STUDENTS

"It is the pupil-teacher idea. It has worked wonderfully and it could be used in any community in the world."

"Describe it for me," I said.

"Well, it goes this way. Here you have the People's School. Let's say there are fifty students in this one class. Out of the fifty you pick, say, about ten, one in every five, who are brighter than the others. These are called guiding students. Now the guiding student does several things. In this particular group of five, while he is still in school, he learns the characters more quickly than the others and so it becomes his duty to help the others. He acts almost as an assistant to the

68

teacher. When he goes home he teaches his family or a class in his neighborhood."

"Don't his fellow students hate him for being superior?" I asked, knowing that human nature anywhere is the same.

But James Yen knows human nature too. "No, because they are selected by their fellow students and not appointed by us. It is all very democratic. You see, they know who are the brightest ones and they choose those. We have a technique so that when a guiding student goes back to his own house he has the method of teaching. He has a simple manual to help him, too, and he knows how to run a small group. Really it is an inspiring sight to see a young boy or girl, sometimes only ten or twelve years old, who is a guiding student. He gathers some old bricks and puts them outdoors in a circle on someone's threshing floor, perhaps, and those who want to learn come and sit on the bricks, sometimes five or six much older people, and the young teacher teaches the whole group. If he is near a teacher he comes back and reports, but the teacher goes around and inspects, in any case.

"Now that system works effectively. It gives the guiding student a chance to review his own lessons; it creates great self-respect in him and a sense of responsibility, too. It teaches, along with school lessons, the necessity of sharing knowledge with others. You can see for yourself that the whole village population soon becomes a student population. Everybody is learning—it becomes the fashion to learn and nobody wants to be left out. There is a community consciousness about learning. The spirit seethes in that village.

"You remember those symbols, five of them, which are enshrined in practically every Chinese home? They are, you remember, these five characters: heaven, earth, king, parent, teacher. Teacher, as you see, is ranked side by side with heaven and earth. The teacher shares the homage and worship of the people with heaven and earth as well as parent and king. That tradition, as you know, accounts for the great reverence that the Chinese people, a farmer or a laborer, have for the scholar, the teacher. So with an educational atmosphere prevailing in the community, everybody wants to learn, and also to teach. No literate who can teach wants to be left out. Indeed it is a privilege to be a student and an honor to be a teacher."

"Are these guiding students paid?" I asked.

"No, it is all voluntary."

"You mean the appeal is only patriotism?"

"Yes," he said simply.

I was not satisfied. "Suppose a guiding student decides it is too much trouble to teach others?"

James Yen was obviously shocked by the idea. "Oh, no, because everybody is in this. It has become what I said—a style, a vogue, a fashion. Now that is what I call education. You create an educational atmosphere. What you teach becomes a habit of the people. That is, education become alive, education vitally rooted."

I saw he was not through and so I listened and did not speak. "Another thing," he went on in his earnest energetic manner. "A very important thing—in this natural and effective way you discover the future leaders of the community. You see, in the first place, those guiding students are elected by their own fellows. In the second place, they have to be good in their work or they won't be elected again. You discover intelligent leadership, then you help develop it. Through service they become leaders. What Christ taught is so true—the greatest among you is the servant of the least of you. That is really the finest pedagogical truth that was ever uttered. These young men and women through serving their community really learn to lead. When this comes about then we have a new technique for training them. We prepare them to be leading farmers—not farm leaders, for that would ruin them, but leading farmers. We don't make them into school teachers, because that would turn their heads. They are still students, although guiding students. They, too, are taught as they teach."

"That is a good distinction," I said, "leading farmers and not farm leaders is what we all want." I thought of our own Pennsylvania farmers who have a fine stubborn quality that reminds me of the Chinese who used to be my neighbors. The other day an expert in

71

soil contour farming visited us and one of our farmers said, "I don't want nobody tellin' me when to plant nor what to plant nor how to plant." But I notice he improves his method very quickly when he sees some other farmer get a better yield than he does.

But you cannot tell James Yen anything about people. He smiled his wise smile. "We train these exceptional young men and women so that they become guides in the community because they are really better farmers than the others."

NEWS, RADIO, THEATRE

"And the Fellow-Scholar Association?" I reminded him.

"Besides teaching many to read, the Fellow-Scholar Association is also responsible for 'wall-news,' " he replied. "That's writing the essential news of the day in chalk on a wall which has been painted black. There were no newspapers for the farmers until the demand for news was so great that we had to run a weekly called 'The Farmer.' It was the first paper ever published for the Chinese farmers in the last three thousand years. The reason is simple. The farmers had never read before.

"Then the radio. We installed a broadcasting station at the county seat, powerful enough to reach the entire county—approximately 400 square miles. The members of the Fellow-Scholar Association had a daily broadcast of useful information about better farming, home improvements, child-care, cooperatives, and health pointers. This began in 1934, when the radio was comparatively new in China and had never been heard of in the rural districts. We had 472 villages but not every village could afford to buy a receiver. We made inexpensive sets and thirty of the larger villages bought them. Each radio receiving station was run by members of the Fellow-Scholar Association. Each day at a regular hour people of the whole village gathered together in front of the receiving station, usually in a temple or an open-air theatre.

"How do our unlettered people know so much about the great events and personalities of Chinese history? It is, as you know, chiefly through the theatre. No matter how poor a village may be you never fail to find an open-air theatre. My colleagues who had specialized in drama made a study of the old Chinese plays. Their aim was to put new spirit and content into the old plays and to write new ones for the people. The Fellow-Scholar Association organized dramatic clubs and theatrical troupes, and traveled from village to village to perform these plays."

I asked about the expense of the troupes.

"To teach the people to read is one thing," James Yen said, "but to bring the schooling within the reach of the people is another thing. Our whole basic Chinese course cost only twelve cents. The same applies

73

to drama. My colleague, Mr. Hsiung, who is one of China's most noted playwrights, found that these young farmers were such adepts in acting that he wanted to write plays for them. With members of the Fellow-Scholar Association he broke down the old conception that acting on the stage is a low profession, and worked out costumes, stage settings and lighting in such a way that they would cost only a few dollars. The troupe is entertained for the day by Fellow-Scholar members of the village or by well-to-do gentry. They travel on foot from one village to another."

SPADE WORK

"Members of the Fellow-Scholar Association worked for such other things as the anti-opium movement, road building and civic improvements in their communities.

"These community leaders do the spade work of reconstruction in community life. That very work provides the content of our schools, the primary schools for children, the people's schools for adults, all adapted to the different grades but teaching the same basic things. The curriculum of the school is the whole reconstruction program and that curriculum is a live one, because while it is teaching and training the young and old it is at the same time reconstructing the village through its activities and projects and spreading out into other villages.

"Take health, for example. Here is this great scourge, smallpox. We say we must prevent smallpox in the class, in the school, in all the schools, and so the smallpox campaign spreads throughout the whole county.

"Or, let us say, this is the time for cotton. Right in class the older farmers are taught some essential modern things about cotton and the younger ones are taught too, and they must go out and help the older ones to practice what they have learned. We have adapted the whole teaching program to the calendar of the farmer. We found that the farmer's lunar calendar is more suitable for his farming. If it is the season for cotton we teach cotton; if it is the right time to tackle smallpox we teach vaccination. In other words, we not only adapt the curriculum to reconstruction, but also we choose the time for teaching that is most effective for the farmer. So you see in each village the school curriculum is related to the whole reconstruction program and everybody is learning and everybody is doing what he learns."

I thought of our little village a mile away. If its two hundred or so people were invaded by, say, the professors and students of the University of Pennsylvania I would not care to answer for the consequences. I asked, "Did the people in Tinghsien object to all these outsiders coming in and tackling their problems, so to speak?"

He gave me that comprehending grin of his. "Well,

by the time we had been there four or five years we had 80,000 'alumni.' So whatever we did was acceptable to those people because we had their confidence and they were a part of us and we of them."

I accepted this and James Yen went on.

MORE INCOME

"Take for example, pigs. Nearly every one of the 68,000 families in the county of Tinghsien keeps a pig. The farmer pays a visit to our agricultural station, where he sees a hog four times as big as his own. This is the Poland-China Grandfather Hog. Then he is shown another, smaller but well built and fat. It is in the same pen with the pig just like his own, which has a sagging back and long bristles that make it look bigger than it really is. He is astonished to learn that these two pigs are the same age and have been fed just the same since birth. The difference is that the bigger one is a cross between the local Northern China pig and the Poland-China. The hybrid, no more expensive to raise, brought the farmer $20 more, which is not to be slighted when his total income for the year was at best about $240—I am speaking of the period before the Sino-Japanese War. The extension of this project alone increased the income of the hsien by a million dollars.

"Take chickens. The Chinese hen lays an average of only 50 eggs a year. By crossing it with white leghorn we got a hen that lays 100. This became popular immediately throughout the district—50 more eggs per hen, at no more cost.

"A farmer named Wu Yu-tien, a member of the Fellow-Scholar Association, worked for three years and developed a strain of wheat that increased the yield per mou by 45 per cent. He is a 'demonstration farmer'—an ordinary farmer persuaded to take up a project on his own land, and so a far better extension agent than the most highly paid expert could be.

"During the winter when the farmers have more leisure our Movement has its golden opportunity. Then the People's Schools are at their height, and then we have a 'Traveling Institute' that goes to various localities and gives intensive training to 'demonstration farmers.' Another thing we do during these so-called 'idle months' is to develop village industries, and Self-Help Societies or cooperatives. We found that two-thirds of the families in Tinghsien were in debt. The city bankers weren't interested in the farmers, yet capital was rotting in the cities for lack of investments. But there were 200 local 'bankers' making loans to the poor farmers at 40 per cent interest. After two years of the Self-Help Societies all of these local 'banks' were closed down. That didn't make us very popular with them. In fact, one night several hundred so-called 'citizens,' tenants and henchmen of the local 'bankers' paraded the streets

77

of Tinghsien shouting in unison, 'Down with the Mass Education Movement.' "

He looked sheepish for a second. Then he laughed and said, "They also yelled, down with me!"

"That was certainly very severe of them," I agreed. "But I daresay you were all popular enough with the people who benefited from those cooperatives."

"Let me tell you a word about the cotton project," he said. "First the cotton farmers produced more cotton because of improved seed, but we found what they gained as better producers, they lost as poor business men. Later all the cotton farmers were trained and they organized their marketing cooperative and shipped their cotton collectively to Tientsin, and sold it directly to the mill owners there. In three years' time their cotton business grew from $120,000 to $1,800,000. No little cotton merchant exploited them. No middleman 'squeezed' them.

"So as a result of fatter pigs, better seeds, smut control, more eggs per hen, cooperatives for credit, marketing and purchasing, the income of the Tinghsien farmer was nearly doubled. If this were applied to all of China and if only one-half of the seventy million farm families used these methods we would have a total increased income of over three billion dollars U.S. currency!

"That is very important, but what is more significant is the training. The fact that farmer Wang is able to produce fifteen per cent more cotton than his ancestors did is a great liberating force in his life. That superstitious mind of his, with its constant fear of demons and evil spirits, is changed into a scientific mind. And he is getting his additional income by cooperating with others. This training in cooperativeness is very essential for a people who are clan-conscious and clan-centered.

"There is much talk nowadays about industrialization in China. I think it is very important. But there is a danger, that we think too much of industrialization without realizing that it depends upon improved farm economy too. For example, one of the reasons why America has such tremendous productive power is the high efficiency of the American farmer. That is a fact many people overlook. Unless the purchasing power of the rural masses is increased, industrialization cannot be supported. Of the millions of people in Asia, over 80 per cent are rural. If the peoples in this rural continent are left in the backwash of primitive farming and illiteracy, they could easily become instruments of dictators aiming at power and conquest. Under such circumstances no industrialization would be practical or beneficial."

LOCAL FINANCING

"Well," I said, "to get back to your demonstration center at Tinghsien, you proved it a success there.

But—can it be financed locally? That is important, else how can you spread the technique everywhere? Not every village or county or even nation has a James Yen."

He waved himself away with a gesture. "Surely finances must be thought of," he said. "Money is needed for the exploration aspect, the primary research experiments, the laboratory work. This has simply to be financed by endowment and contributions.

"But this money is needed only for the primary experimental stage of the work. The stage of application and extension can usually be financed locally. The people themselves are willing to pay for what they get. What actually happened in Tinghsien was this. We financed the first two experimental schools and six demonstration schools. But the 472 People's Schools resulting from these first eight schools were all financed and manned by the people themselves. This is typical."

"Did they pay fees?" I asked.

"They did not," he said. "They decided themselves not to have fees but to raise the money in other ways. But again I must remind you of an important financial principle of this whole education for the people—it must be fundamentally within the economic range of the people, so that it is something they can pay for. Of course, if the government decides to apply it on a larger scale, then it can be paid for by taxes."

"All this work was private and not governmental," I said. "Did the government of China pay no heed to what you were doing for national reconstruction?"

James Yen looked quizzical. "I did not want too much government at first, especially during the earlier years when we did not have a unified national government. We wanted to be free to try out our plans and to uphold our intellectual integrity. We conducted a second experimental center in Hunan, Central China, then a third one in Szechwan, West China. We tried out these experiments in typical regions, under varying conditions, so that we could evolve something that would be nationally applicable. Our aim was for the nation all the time, though we worked in different localities."

The library where we had been talking all morning was very quiet as James Yen said these words. We had been talking a long time, but neither of us was tired. The sun had climbed to high noon and the walnut tree outside the window stood in a round pool of its own shade. James Yen was looking out and beyond the shadow, over sunlit hills that led to the horizons of the world.

"All this which you have done in China can be used in the world," I said.

"Yes," he replied, simply.

The one word was so final that it put a period to the morning. As though the whole house felt it the big bell on the porch began to clang for dinner. The silence was broken by the sound of children's feet and voices. We came back from our journey over the earth and were home again in a Pennsylvania farm house.

But we were not finished. "Tomorrow?" I asked. "Tomorow," he promised.

CHAPTER TWO

AN AWAKENING

THE NEXT MORNING he came into the library as though in the intervening afternoon and night he had done nothing but think. He had a list of memoranda in his hand and he held it purposefully. But I knew he had walked and played tennis and gone swimming and helped to cook Sunday supper because we had all done these things together. Certainly he had not lain awake sleepless. He looked too alive for that this morning. But James Yen has lived this work of his so long that now it has become his life. Whatever else he does is on the surface of himself—give him a moment and the bottom comes boiling up.

"When I got thinking of all we talked about yesterday," he began, "I felt that I hadn't made you understand the most wonderful part of it all to me, myself. It was the discovery of our own people. That was true for the whole group of intellectuals who worked in the people's education movement in China. We were so stirred, so inspired, by the splendid qualities of our own common people that we just had to do something about them. The first step, you see, was really an awakening of the intellectuals. It all came out of that. I feel that is what is needed everywhere, this awakening of the privileged, whether the privileged in education or in wealth. And then the next step was not to copy slavishly anybody else but to learn of the people themselves, what they wanted and could use. We soon learned that whatever we did we had to make it simple—simple for the teacher to teach and simple for the student to learn. It had to be economical, too, economical of time, for the people haven't much time, and economical of money, for the people haven't much money."

I asked him, "Did it occur to you, in those first days, that you were working on a world problem when you tried to solve the problems of your own country?"

James Yen answered gravely: "No. We were just thinking in terms of China and trying to work out methods to meet China's needs. For instance, we did not recommend the abolition of the Chinese characters. We made use of them. There is a tradition behind our characters. But we simplified the learning of those characters so that an average man can learn to read and write easily. In other words, we learned to utilize the best of our heritage. This, by the way, is an important principle to bear in mind in undertaking social reconstruction in any nation."

PEOPLE'S LITERATURE

"After we had taught them to read and write we were faced with the problem of providing reading material for them. China has a rich literature but it is written in *wen-li*, the classical medium, and is therefore not for the masses. The drama was democratic and available for all, but literature was for the aristocracy of scholars. Even the *pai-hua* literature now being published is still primarily for the intellectuals and student class, and is far beyond the reach of the masses, in both vocabulary and content. So our Department of People's Literature went to work writing stories and other literature for the people.

"They had a great deal of difficulty. They had been trained in the classical school. In writing for the people, they must change their standards altogether, and achieve simplicity of expression and directness of appeal, with the limitations imposed by the life experiences of their new reading public.

"The creation of a people's literature was approached scientifically; the writers were trained in the use of the language and they studied at first hand the people for whom they were to write. The subjects were stories from Chinese history, general information about modern China, lives of great men and

85

women of China and other nations, simple accounts of scientific discoveries, descriptions of methods of improving agricultural production, information about common ailments and other health knowledge, plays, poems and songs."

"Of course you had the traditional techniques of the traveling theatres and the wandering story-tellers to help you," I reminded him. I myself, as a child growing up in the Chinese countryside, had learned my first history and literature from the tongues of the story-tellers on the streets and the plays on the hillsides before the temples.

"We made a special research study of folk songs and folk literature," he replied. "These are the real living literature of the people. Never written down, but passed on from generation to generation. We had to get those who were familiar with them to recite or sing them while our writers took them down, word for word. Studies of this sort helped to bring our writers to a better understanding of the culture of our race. In folk literature they found a great deal that was fine and true and representative of the best qualities of the Chinese.

"The Fellow-Scholar Association had the job of getting these books to the rural people. They organized reading clubs and conducted traveling libraries to bring the books to them. There is now a 'People's Library' of over a thousand volumes on all subjects, and these books are sold at a price the farmer can afford.

"So also through drama and painting and folk art we explored China's long past.

"Our Art Department selected our national heroes and heroines, who embodied the best qualities of the race. Large paintings of those national heroes were prepared for the People's Schools. With each painting was a couplet summing up the greatness of the character, which the students committed to memory; and in addition there was a song written about the same personality which the students learned to sing.

"History is the most valuable material which is given to a nation for the fashioning of its future. We taught it not by the usual copying of beautiful ideas and ideals as expressed in the classics, but through national ideals as actually lived by men and women of flesh and blood in China's history."

PUBLIC HEALTH

"But what about public health?" I said. "It's a very new subject, and western in origin. Did you take our American pattern and apply it to China?"

"No, like education we have to work it out in our own way. In this great country you have one physician for every 800 of population. China has one modern trained physician for every 70,000 of population! And if we aim to have only one physician for

87

every 2,000 population, we shall need about 225,000 physicians. At the present rate of medical training, it would take 450 years! We have to find something that can be done under the present circumstances.

"We have two rather simple but important tests for all our work. One is, can the people do it? The other is, can the people pay for it? We must start with where the farmer is today. In West China we call a poor man a 'water-rice' eater and the well-to-do, a 'steamed rice' eater. Americans are enjoying 'steamed rice' in public health, but what we tried to do in China was to give our people at least the 'water rice' in public health."

"Even 'water-rice' saves lives," I put in, and remembered the sorrow of children and strong young men and women dying before their time of diseases which here in America we know are not fatal.

"We found that nearly thirty per cent of the people who died in Tinghsien received no medical attention whatsoever, and 220 of the 472 villages in the hsien had no medical facilities of any kind. The other 252 villages had 'doctors,' who prescribed drugs which they themselves sold, and not infrequently they were illiterates.

"There was little knowledge of contagion or isolation of infectious diseases. In the delivery of a child, mud was often used to stop the bleeding of the cord. People drank water from wells just a few feet from unprotected latrines. Children with diphtheria and scarlet fever lay in the same bed with the healthy children of the family. Tetanus and smallpox were responsible for a large number of deaths every year.

"That poverty and ignorance are among the chief causes of disease in any country can scarcely be disputed. It's obvious then that any attempt to improve the health of the farmer without simultaneous efforts to raise the standard of livelihood and general education would surely fail.

"Here in America you have a situation which we in China hope to avoid. You developed medicine first and public health later and as a result you have two distinct branches always in friction with one another and this is wasteful of money and personnel. We believe that we should have these two combined into one system. The medical student must be trained in both curative and preventive medicine at the same time and take responsibility for both. This will save both money and personnel. I cannot emphasize too much that unless you can be economical in these two matters you won't have anything that can be universalized among the people.

"It's also obvious that for some years to come it will be impossible for the average Chinese village to have a qualified doctor or a qualified nurse. The solution as we see it lies in making the villagers themselves aware of their problem, arousing in them a sense of responsibility for it, and giving them the necessary training to work on it. We used laymen in the

89

villages as the foundation of our community health system."

"Not having doctors to oppose it, no one is offended, I suppose."

James Yen gave one of his quick smiles. "No one," he agreed, "and there is even honor in it."

"The village health worker is a Fellow-Scholar and is elected by the Association. He gets a brief concentrated course of training at the 'ch'u' or sub-hsien Health Station. He is trained to do five things. One, record the births and deaths of his village; two, vaccinate against smallpox and cholera; three, give simple treatments out of his Health Protection Box, which contains sixteen essential and safe drugs, including ointment for the treatment of trachoma, disinfectants and some sterilized bandages; four, give health talks with demonstrations and charts prepared by the Health Department; and five, maintain a sanitary well in the village. It's amazing to see the amount of good that a Health Worker can do in a village where no medical facilities ever existed before."

"Do you pay the Health Worker?" I asked.

"No, he is a volunteer. He has his own farming to attend to, but at certain times of the day he opens up the clinic. In case of emergency someone rushes to his field or his home to get him. As he is elected by his Fellow-Scholars, it's a great honor for him to be a Health Worker. And of course he is a nephew or a cousin or some kind of relative to other members of the community. He takes great pride in giving his service free. But the time when he gets special compensation and recognition is the Chinese New Year. Then the people have the village teacher write three or four characters on a red paper scroll to express the appreciation of the community. They present the scroll to the village Health Worker together with one or two pounds of pork while fire-crackers are shot off. Probably the whole performance won't cost the village more than a dollar but it means a lot to the Health Worker. In fact, his is a very enviable position, almost like a *hsiu ts'ai* ('budding genius') degree in the old Imperial Civil Service Examination days!

"The Health Worker has his technical limitations. So the sub-hsien Health Station, staffed with a physician and a dresser, is in a centrally located village. It trains and supervises the Health Workers in as many as fifty villages, conducts lectures on health, and attends to patients passed on by the village Health Workers.

"Then as a sort of health power house for the entire hsien there is a Health Center, with a hospital and laboratory, offices and classrooms. It trains the workers of the sub-hsien Health Stations and gives physicians supplementary training. Other lines of work at the center are studies of rural health problems, epidemic control, school health, training of mid-wives, and birth control.

"We found it possible to give a minimum of medical relief and health protection to the 400,000 population in the hsien at a total cost of around $36,000, or ten cents per capita!"

NEW CITIZENSHIP

James Yen paused a moment, then he said, "Now let me go back. By the end of 1936, Tinghsien had a relatively high proportion of literacy, and a leaven of 80,000 young men and women with a knowledge of their won language and culture, their imaginations stirred by new ideas, their patriotism kindled, and a new cooperative spirit developed. It had a population with its economic level raised to make possible the taking of thought for something besides filling the rice bowl. A population like that was ready to learn the meaning of citizenship.

"Mr. Chen Chu-san, Head of the Department of Citizenship Training, had been carrying on a study of village self-government as it had been for centuries, to see how it could be adapted to modern Chinese democracy. Mr. Chen has behind him long years of scholarship of the old type, bitter political experience in the early days of the Revolution, prolonged exile and study in Japan, and teaching in Chinese universities which he felt were not as yet expressive of the genius of the Chinese people. With such a rich background, Mr. Chen's study resulted in a simple system which may be called a 'philosophy of co-operative living,' and forms the basis for good citizenship. Briefly, the core of this system is 'family concord,' which gradually widens out to include the village, then extends beyond the village through hsien and province until it takes in the nation, and finally 'all under heaven, in one family.' *Ta Chia*, the Chinese expression 'everybody,' means literally 'the Great Family.'

"Mr. Chen's experiment village was comparatively enlightened, having a Primary School and five People's Schools of different grades for men and women. But its predominating clan was split up in factions that had not even been on speaking terms for several years. They were very bitter, though they scarcely knew why. Little by little they began to see the absurdity of the situation. After months of effort on Mr. Chen's part, the leaders of the factions met for dinner at his home and talked over the steps that might be taken for civil improvement.

"They were faced with a practical problem. The net resources of the village, after legitimate and illegitimate taxes had been paid, amounted to $220. Out of this sum all civic expenditures, including education, must be met. Obviously, the village could not build fine roads, or an elaborate sanitation system, or support a nurse or a policeman or a fire brigade. But it

93

could go to school, and it could organize. Of the village population of about seven hundred, more than half have now studied in our schools. They have been imbued with ideas which lead beyond any boundaries they had known heretofore. Training in cooperation is constantly emphasized in the Thousand Character Lessons, the follow-up literature, and the activities of the People's Schools. In the 'Better Homes' Club, familiar abuses and disgraces take on a new and intolerable aspect, and they find that something can be done about them. In the 'Love My Village' Club, they begin to get a sense of pride in their village—how can they beautify it? How can they add to its well-being? This is the first step towards patriotism, which is so much talked about in China and so little understood.

"This experiment in village citizenship is chiefly significant in that it is not imposed from above to accord with the pre-conceived ideas of a political theorist, but is a natural development of the whole program of the Tinghsien Experiment. It would have little vitality or effectiveness without the educational, economic, and health work, and these, in turn, would lose much of their meaning if they could not be integrated in this conception of new citizenship."

"Your program," I said, "as it grows out of the village, sounds highly practical, but could you carry it out under the old hsien system of government?"

"That is a very ticklish question," said James Yen, smiling.

THE FOURTH LEG

"The hsien magistrate has been called traditionally the 'parent official,' but alas, he has been more of a tyrant than a parent. You remember the story about Confucius and the peasant woman? Confucius one day saw a woman weeping by the side of the road. 'Why do you weep?' asked the Sage. She replied, 'I weep because my father was killed a year ago by a tiger. A year after that my brother was killed by a tiger. Then last month my husband was carried away by a tiger. And today, a tiger has eaten my only son.' The old Sage was puzzled, and said: 'Why don't you move to some other place where there are no man-eating tigers?' The woman replied: 'Oh Master, I wouldn't move, because there is no oppressive government here.'

"The farmer doesn't care much as to who is a cabinet minister or the governor of the province, but he does care who is the magistrate of his hsien, whether he is good or bad. The functions of the hsien government have been for centuries to collect taxes and to try civil suits and criminals. We determined to have this antiquated machinery reorganized. We were treading on dangerous ground, when so many little potentates had a stake in the status quo. Yet as one of our ancient wise men said: 'Unless you enter the tiger's den, you cannot get the cubs.' It is easy to criticize the hsien government, but what did we really know about the difficulties? We realized that unless we ourselves entered into the government and served as magistrates and bureau heads, taking up the actual problems, we would not know how to reform it."

"But how could you do such a thing as private individuals?" I asked.

"That's just it. How could a group of scholars get control of the hsien government? In the fall of 1932 the Central Government sent Mr. Kan Nai-kwang, the Vice Minister of the Interior, on an extensive tour of the country to find out whether there were methods developed anywhere that would help bring to realization the ideal of hsien self-government as advocated by Dr. Sun Yat-sen. Mr. Kan intended to stay in Tinghsien for just one day, but he became so interested that he stayed four days, and twice our evening talks lasted until two in the morning.

"What he said to me was this, 'Your program here for social reconstruction is practical and effective, but it's just like a square table with only three legs—the educational, the economic, and the health—and you need one more leg, the political leg, to make the table stand up straight.' "

"We sat up a couple of nights to draw up a plan for the fourth leg. Then Mr. Kan made a strong recommendation to the Central Government, which called a National Conference on Home Affairs. The

Conference decided that the provinces should establish Institutes and experimental hsien to study the problem of hsien government and initiate reforms from the bottom up instead of from the top down. I was asked to be the president of the Institute of Political Reconstruction for the province in which Tinghsien is situated, and given authority to recommend personnel for the hsien government. I capitalized on this and chose several of my most experienced colleagues to serve as magistrate and bureau heads.

THE TIGER'S DEN

"So at last we actually entered the tiger's den! But we found it was not easy to get the cubs. We learned what it was to arouse bitter jealousies. People who had been merely indifferent became our enemies. But through many trials and struggles we developed a new organization for the hsien government, and converted it from an agency chiefly for taxation and litigation to one working for the welfare of the people. We put in public health, adult education, agriculture, cooperatives, as integral functions of the hsien government.

"What is most gratifying is this, that after the people had learned to run their own People's Schools, their modern farms, their cooperatives, their health clinics, they demanded that they should run their own government! Is there anything more natural and more inevitable? After all, what is government for? Is it not an agency for the welfare of the people? What is the welfare of the people? Education, livelihood and health. So, people who have learned to run their own education, livelihood, and health are the very people who are competent to run their own government. People talk about self-government as if it were entirely a thing in itself, apart from other aspects of life. To me self-government is the inevitable result of a people who are educated and capable of carrying on their own social and economic welfare.

"As I pointed out before we conducted another experiment in Hengshan, Hunan, in Central China, and a third in Hsin-tu, in Szechwan, West China, for all the time we were thinking of China as a whole.

"Hsin-tu is our youngest experimental hsien. Being the youngest, it has the advantage of drawing upon the experiences of the older hsien. So within the short period of eighteen months it made a fine and widely recognized record in local government administration, finance, land-registration, people's militia and population census. The last three mentioned are the new features of this experimental hsien. When we first selected Hsin-tu we were told there was on the average one case of kidnapping every week. The Fellow-Scholars Association organized a People's Militia, for self defense against bandits, and to cooperate with the rural police (which was also reformed). Banditry soon disappeared. During the whole eighteen months only two cases of robbery were reported, and in each case the culprits were arrested within two hours. Besides giving security to the people, this new People's Militia resulted in a net savings of $7000 in the budget provided for the old Public Safety Corps. And the people used this fund for supporting the Hsien Health Center."

A CENSUS

"Now a word about population census. China's population has been quoted variously as from 350 million to 500 million. Really we are extremely hazy about it. If you ask anyone in China the exact figure. I don't believe he can tell you. Even a hsien does not know its population. So a census, we felt, must be a basic part of our program. However, 'counting heads' is a delicate matter because the villagers resent it. Again the Fellow-Scholars play an important role. Together with primary school teachers, trained in the essentials of census taking, they carried out the whole project. That was the first scientific census ever taken of any hsien in Szechwan Province and that was in 1936."

"It's a real step forward to get people to be willing to give you facts about themselves for a census," I observed. Actually I was too polite to say that I did not blame them. They were too often taxed by local warlords after such questionings. No wonder population figures were hazy!

"If we are hazy about our population figures, we are worse about our land." James Yen went on. "No hsien knows how much land it has. To launch a land survey project for Hsin-tu all the available forces of the hsien were mobilized, with the Fellow-Scholars taking the lead. The survey revealed an apparent increase of 66,000 mou of rice field alone! This discovery of 'new' rice land indicates both ignorance and negligence on the part of the government officials as well as evasion of the land tax by the powerful gentry. A list of the lots of the 'black' lands and their owners was published. You can see how this work helps to lay the foundation for an equitable land tax, which in the past had been a source of injustice to the people, and of corruption among the officials. Of all the three experimental hsien the Movement conducted in China, Hsin-tu created the largest number of enemies for the Movement."

"What kind of enemies did you create," I asked, anxious to know who could oppose James Yen.

"We created all kinds of enemies and some terrible things happened," he replied seriously. "Through the People's Militia we cleaned out the bandits and the old Police Force. Through the Land Survey we exposed the 'black' land of the landed gentry and local warlords. Later on the word got round that the provincial government would adopt these systems for the whole of Szechwan Province. So, what happened? One night over a thousand 'citizens' gathered at the city gates and surrounded the city wall of Hsin-tu and yelled, 'Down with the Experiment Hsien. Down with the magistrate!' The next night the same thing, one thousand more 'citizens' surrounded the town and demanded that the magistrate be dismissed. We had at the time an illiterate soldier as governor. He succumbed to the pressure of the gang and had the magistrate dismissed.

"A year or so later the Generalissimo took over the administration of the province and when he learned about this Hsin-tu 'incident' he was indignant. It was not long after this that he recommended the New Hsien Government System for the whole of China."

"The Generalissimo has often shown interest in your work?" I interposed. During the conversation I had more than once wanted to ask the question.

"Yes," James Yen said modestly. "After he first heard about the Tinghsien experiment, he sent one of his close associates, General Chang Chi-chung, to come to see it.

"The Generalissimo, who was then chairman of the State Council, asked me to go down to Nanking to see him. We spent one afternoon and two evenings in succession discussing the Tinghsien work and how it could be applied to rural reconstruction in China. Madame Chiang was present at every talk and was most enthusiastic. The Generalissimo called a special meeting of the entire staff and cadets of the Central

Military Academy to hear me. The Generalissimo presided. I confess I was quite long-winded. I talked over two hours to more than 2000 instructors and cadets all standing. You know the Generalissimo is a man of few words, but after my two hours' talk he spoke for another three-quarters of an hour!

"Among other things he said to the cadets: 'If you young men are to do your part to awaken the masses as Dr. Sun taught, then you must learn the practical methods and ways of doing it. The Tinghsien experiment has pointed out to you the way of doing it. What is even more important than method is the spirit of the Tinghsien workers. They are scholars and scientists but they don't stay in the comfortable cities, they go to the poor villages, and live and work with the people. It is that spirit of serving the people that is going to save our country. So I want to send you all to Tinghsien to learn the method and to catch the spirit!'

"As it was impossible to send such a large number, the Generalissimo selected representative groups and sent them to Tinghsien where each stayed for six weeks."

BLAZING NEW TRAILS

"But you have kept your Movement out of politics," I said.

"Yes, if you want to have freedom to experiment, you must keep out of politics," he replied, "That applies to China and I think it applies everywhere. The government could help you with subsidies, but they should not give you so much that they control your whole program."

"What about America where the people elect their own government?" I asked him.

"No, not even in America," James Yen said firmly. "You see, ever so many private institutions here are doing really creative work and are much ahead of the government. They are leading the government and blazing new trails all the time. I think that even in your country if you want to initiate new ideas and new systems in education or in other fields you had better remain non-political so that you can have absolute freedom to experiment. It is the only way to preserve your intellectual integrity. Otherwise, you will be lost through compromises."

He paused and began again. "Another thing—it was so heartening to see the people capable of taking care of themselves after what they had learned had become a part of their lives. When people are able to reconstruct their own environment, then any kind of social or political or economic reforms that are launched begin to take root because the people get hold of them. After the foundation training and basic discipline, they know how to struggle with problems, they are no longer helpless in the face of catastrophe, they grow with strength. That is the way a nation develops.

"What our specialists must do is to find the essence of what the people need to know and to do. The people have no time to learn this and that. They need desperately, with their little time and little money, to learn exactly the right things. You undoubtedly know that legend of the wise old man. People came to ask him about the way to immortality. He told them to gather all the herbs of the world and put them in a cauldron and boil them down until all that is left is the essence of all those herbs. Then you make a little pill out of that, and if you ate it you would achieve immortality.

"Now that is the essence of essences—it is a process, and it ought to give us a clear idea of what to do first for the people. They have no time for quantitative education and so whatever we give them must be qualitative, the very essence of the most vital knowledge, so that they learn something important every time we teach them. That is education at its best. That is what we want for the world as a whole. Make the essential knowledge available *for* the people and applicable *by* the people. This calls for creative researchers."

INTEGRATED APPROACH

He was on his feet and pacing the room again. "But I mustn't forget to tell you the all-important principle of *correlation* in this whole business of social reconstruction. Life is an organic whole. It should not be 'compartmentalized.' When you think of the 'four root evils' we have been discussing, you cannot help seeing their inter-locking character. Poverty, for example, is a cause of disease; disease and ill-health are economically wasteful and so a cause of poverty. Poverty and disease are in turn both largely a result of ignorance. And unless there is an effective political system in which the people are capable of participating, very little of permanent value can be accomplished along cultural, economic and health lines. So, when we talk about the 'four fundamentals' of social reconstruction, they are not pigeon-holes to divorce aspetcs of life that are related. They are merely a convenient way of organizing a very complex program. That is why we emphasize a *correlated* program rather than an isolated approach. Education, economic improvement, public health and self-government are so interrelated and mutually dependent that the *success of one depends upon the success of the other*."

TWO CEREMONIES

"People seem to think if they build a school they have done everything necessary. They pay no attention to what is taught or how it is taught. Let me tell you a little story about a very influential friend of mine. He was a high official and had a genuine love for the people of his home town. He knew about the work of Tinghsien. One day, he asked me: 'Yen,

105

won't you come to my district and help start an experimental center? Make it a model district in this part of our country.' I said: 'I would be glad to go and see what kind of place you have.' So I went.

"The town's main street was paved. It was a fine-looking street, but the houses on both sides were just as poor as those in any other village. The village school was a modern building, an imposing place. It cost several hundred thousand dollars! The principal took me round the school, and I saw a whole row of rooms all locked up. They had glass windows, so I peeped in and saw what they were—modern flush toilets.

"I asked the school principal: 'Why is this nice place all locked up?'

"He was much embarrassed. He said, 'The children don't know how to use them and they would go to a corner until the whole place smelled, and so we had to lock up the toilets.'

"The next day happened to be the anniversary of Dr. Sun's death. The school held a memorial service and all the children, about three hundred of them, came in their nice little uniforms and caps. After a solemn ceremony, the school gave each of the little boys and girls one little tree, a seedling, and they all went out and planted the trees.

"Now—by an irony of fate—in the afternoon something else went on in the community. It had its own celebrations, and that day happened to be the birthday of their idol. It was the custom to carry out the idol in a very beautiful sedan chair, and parade the streets. I went out to see the procession. I was amused to see that the four little attendants to the idol walking just next to the sedan chair were little school boys. They wore long robes over their uniforms, yellow silk robes, dirty, from long use. And in front of the sedan chair were forty or fifty other little boys, all dressed up like demons or ghosts, dancing around, and they also had their costumes over their uniforms.

"Scores of little children carried by their mothers watched the procession. As the idol in its sedan chair passed by, the mothers would pull their little one's sleeves and say, 'Worship the god! Worship the god!' After the parade was over and the village quiet again, I joined the boys sitting on the street pavement. I asked them why they worshipped the idol. One of the boys volunteered the answer: 'My mother said that if you don't worship the idol you will get ill.' "

HOME EDUCATION

"I went back and reported to my friend. I pointed out that what I had seen proved the big gap between our school education and home education. I said, 'Just school education is not enough; there must be home education; there must be community education. In the morning the teachers taught modern things such as tree-planting on the anniversary of Dr. Sun's death. But in the afternoon the community got the children to celebrate the birthday of the idol. In the home, the mother, inculcates her own theory of preventing diseases in the children. There's the teaching of the school, there's the teaching of the home and the community.' My friend became greatly embarrassed. 'Anyway,' I said, 'that's not only true of your district. It's typical of the whole country.

" 'The school is not the only channel of education,' I told him. 'There is the home and the community and you must educate the people through all three.' This is what we mean in Tinghsien by the 'Four Fundamentals of Reconstruction' and 'Three Types of Education'. The cultural, economic, health and political form the *content;* the school, the home and the community are the *channels* of integration.

" 'You have education and reconstruction proceeding through one another by means of one another. When you have finished the job of education you have done the job of reconstruction.' "

TEAMWORK

I saw this plan of education bringing forth a reconstructed world as he talked. Then I thought of men and how they are and I asked another question.

"But all these things must be done through human beings. Did you find these men always willing, always faithful, always filled with your own zeal? Didn't you find that there were people who would not cooperate? What did you do with them—eliminate them?"

A certain tired look passed over James Yen's face. "No, but I tell you, the personnel was one of my most important jobs. It is comparatively—I will say only comparatively—easy to get first-rate men. They are rare animals, but it is possible to find them. But it is not easy or simple to get first-rate men to work together. Because they are creative, they are individualistic, stubborn, and think all the world of themselves and little of others. They stick persistently to their own opinions and refuse to accept other people's points of view. You have no idea—" he stopped and shook his head.

"I think I have," I said, laughing a little.

James Yen joined in my laughter ruefully. "Well, you see, we demanded so much of our workers and colleagues and we gave them so little money. They came to work with us for one-third of what they had been getting and some had large families. It was very difficult, sometimes. I would say that one-fourth of my own time was spent in lubrication. You have no idea how some of the older members, who ought to be mature and able to work with others, behaved. But their experience had never called for team work, and so when such men came to us I had to talk correlation every minute.

"There was a man in our department of literature, for example. In order that he might be able to write interestingly, he had to know the people in our agricultural department and learn the agricultural needs of the farmers. He had to know the people in the education department and learn some of the problems that the educational men had, and what were the weaknesses and strong points of students. In other words, that man, even though he was a member of the Literature Department, had to cooperate with the members of every other department and learn from them, and they from him. Well, usually those scholars think, 'Oh, I can write well, my style is good,'—you know the Chinese scholar—'My style is good; why should I go,' and so forth, and as a result, he never writes anything of real content or interest to the farmers. It was of no use. Beautiful style minus content may be all right for the scholar, but not for the farmer!"

RE-EDUCATING THE EDUCATED

I had a little speech of my own to make and I made it now. "As I have been listening to you talk, I keep thinking all the time, not of Tinghsien, but of Tinghsien applied to the world and not only to one nation. But what you are calling for here in your correlated program is a type of individual who has to be educated to team work. If you gave a fourth of your time to lubrication in Tinghsien, who is going to spend time lubricating all over the world, so to speak? There has got to be something more than you, even. Now we can say in the demonstration center of these first People's Schools you take what you can get, you take a college president, you take a great scientist, you take so and so. You must for the sake of demonstration get them to work together, as you probably do; but as you train people to go out and be leaders, as this program reflects back into the university so that the university begins training people for the program, then an integral part of that program has to be team work; you have to train college professors and scientists to think in terms of a correlated program and to be able to do team work."

"You are right," James Yen said. "But you must also instill into them the spirit of service and self-sacrifice. They have to learn to 'step down' too. My colleague Professor Yao was a case in point. He studied in Michigan and Wisconsin, and he went back and later became dean of his college in Peking. I talked to him. 'Now, what about coming down to Tinghsien and see what you can do for the farmers?' He resigned and came. He was very much interested in what we were doing in agriculture. I said, 'I would like to see you try one thing; you organize a cooperative and have these newly-taught literate members participate in it, and then out of the good members, fifty or sixty, elect officers. You must require that the officers can do everything, bookkeeping and whatnot, and I want you to evolve a system of accounting that these alumni, the officers of the cooperatives, can make use of so they can keep accounts themselves instead of depending upon highly-trained men.'

"He said, 'I will try.' That man conducted all the farmers' circulating institutes from one village center to another, and he ran the credit cooperatives. The credit cooperatives are simple, but when you come to marketing cooperatives, purchasing cooperatives, co-operative banking, then it is not so simple. He supervised them all. In a typical cooperative, which one finds in the villages, usually only one or two members can read or write and can keep accounts, and the temptation is strong for the few to exploit all the rest.

"You won't find this in Tinghsien. Because the majority of the cooperative members are graduates of the People's Schools and are Fellow-Scholars, each is anxious to have the approval of his fellows, and they have mutual feelings; so all these things go back to that main beginning of the training. After three years our friend was able to evolve an accounting system that is adapted to the needs of the various kinds of cooperatives, marketing cooperatives or purchasing cooperatives. He was a great professor and the dean of a college, and knew higher mathematics and economics. But he had to step down and work out something that could be used and put into practice by simple farmers. That's the final test: can the farmers use it?"

I could see that James Yen was done with this. A dreaming speculative look flitted across his face. It passed and he jumped to his feet and began walking around. "I was told that at a meeting in Washington last week, they were talking about reconstruction work after rehabilitation in Asia, and somebody objected and said that education was too slow, something else was needed. Then another member spoke up. He was a distinguished professor and had personally visited Tinghsien. He told the group about how we had improved the hogs and the chickens and how we brought in goats for milk—a cow is too big and cumbersome for the average Chinese farm family— and he told about the improvement in cotton and millet and about the cooperatives, the credit cooperatives where the farmers could borrow at a low rate of interest and the marketing cooperatives where the farmer could sell his produce profitably.

"And then he said: 'In Tinghsien education was for reconstruction and reconstruction through education. Education being slow didn't apply there. Well, you know the average farm family of Tinghsien, which was typical, was making an income of about $240, Chinese currency, a year round 1930. After the improvements, he was making twice as much with little additional expense, chiefly by improving his animal stock, his seeds, his methods of production and cooperative organization. Then the higher health rate meant fewer funerals—funerals in China are expensive, and they didn't marry so early and had less expensive weddings. And last but not least, there was developed a government in Tinghsien that cost less to maintain and was more useful to the people and did not take such high taxes. It's not easy to put these benefits in terms of dollars and cents but they contribute materially to the farmer's general prosperity. Now, just multiply that additional income by 35 million farm families, that would bring in about three billion dollars extra spending money to the nation.'

"After twenty years, we know we can make this program work, and in ten years' time wipe out illiteracy and double the farmer's income. And after people have received that fourfold, integrated training in education, livelihood, health and self-government, a firm foundation will be laid for a great, modern China, and that is what we are after. Our primary interest is in creating a new people. That is fundamental."

GUERRILLA GOVERNMENT

He stopped dreaming and sat down. "The war didn't stop our work," he began again. "Because of the war, its progress has been accelerated in a number of ways."

He laughed. "You know, of all the guerrilla divisions in Northern China they tell us that the one in

Tinghsien is the most ferocious. The government sent men to make some investigations in the north. One of them came back and told us what he found the Tinghsien lads were actually doing. They were not only running both guerrilla warfare and local reconstruction at the same time in their own district, but were the leaders for all the neighboring counties. Of the 472 villages of Tinghsien, the enemy was able to occupy only 21, and these were along the railroad. Either side of the railroad the enemy dared not penetrate. The rest of the villages were under the supervision of two magistrates elected by the people. The magistrate of a section east of the railroad was a former teacher of the People's School, and the magistrate of the western section was a graduate of the People's School. The people of Tinghsien are carrying on!

"I was much heartened when I heard all this. After all, what it does indicate is not so much that those Tinghsien young men and women are able to carry on the guerrilla warfare and reconstruction of their county, as the fact that the methods, the content as evolved in Tinghsien, in training these young people have proved their effectiveness. They have proved indestructible."

MOBILIZING FOR DEFENSE

"After the war began the Governor of Hunan Province, General Chang, sent for me. Chang is an old friend and a staunch supporter of the Movement. As I said, he had three years before the war visited Tinghsien on behalf of the Generalissimo. Here is the gist of what he said: 'Now, Yen, I have a difficult and urgent job. I have been entrusted with the task of mobilizing the 30 million people of this province to resist the invader and I need all the help I can get. Can you give us any suggestions?'

"I said, 'There is one thing we know, and that is if we want to mobilize the people of Hunan, we must first win their confidence. If we want to win their confidence, we must see to it that they have at least an honest and efficient hsien government, which is the government that is closest to the life of the people. That is where we ought to start. Now to do that, we must do two things. First, reorganize the hsien government. Hitherto it has been mainly an agency for collecting taxes, trying law suits, keeping the peace. Now we must convert it into an agency for carrying out people's education, people's livelihood, people's health, and people's government, as well as for training and mobilizing the people for resistance. This new government needs new men to run it. Its vital that we re-train the civil service men in the province from the magistrates down to the village heads.'

"He said, 'Your ideas agree completely with mine and what I plan to do: but I have one important thing to ask of you: Will you take the responsibility of carrying out this program?' That was a great challenge to me. I didn't want to get mixed up with politics. I had steered clear of it for years. But a war was on. And Chang is a statesman and one of the ablest and finest men I have come to know in our country. So, I accepted and offered to serve as a volunteer worker. In fact, later, our entire staff then in Hunan threw themselves unreservedly into the work.

"We realized that we had to inject new blood into the service. It so happened at that time tens of thousands of refugees had come from the coast provinces to Hunan and a number of them were educated men and women, college professors, students, professionals, school teachers, and social workers. Some 5000 of these were enlisted and trained for the higher offices of the hsien government. We divided up the province of Hunan into three regions, according to emergency. The region of greatest emergency was the one which the Japanese would reach soonest; the second was one of less emergency; the third region was much less urgent. For the first region concentrated training was given to the magistrates, bureau heads, and village elders in only six weeks; for the second region we had six months, and for the third, one year."

TEAM TRAINING

"The men and women were organized into classes according to their functions, and were given special training accordingly. Then at the end of each week, taking the hsien, or county, as a unit the various officers and members of the hsien government came to meet and discuss the agricultural, educational and health problems and the most effective means of mobilizing the people of the hsien to which they were assigned. The magistrate was the chairman and led the discussion, assisted by his bureau heads, and co-ordinated the various activities of his hsien. Instead of talking about abstract subjects, these men took up the actual problems facing their own hsien. They all shared a common plan and each knew what each was supposed to do and also how each was supposed to work with other members in the hsien.

"When they were through with the training they were already a team. They were sent to their hsien not as strangers to one another or isolated individuals, as has always been the case in the past, but they went as *one team*. Now, that team-training has been recognized as one of the significant features in the whole civil service program. All the seventy-five hsien governments of the province were reorganized. That was the most thorough-going social and political reorganization that ever took place in our country.

"Altogether we trained 5000 higher officers and

30,000 village heads. But in training village heads, we went to their own village centers. That was one of those things we took special care in avoiding, taking them away from their own farms, from their own homes. We went where they were. The Japanese had been wanting to capture that province for a long, long time. When they made the attack the first time they were driven back; then the second time, they were driven back, and the third time, driven back. The commanders in those military campaigns said their victories were, in no small measure, due to the effective cooperation of the hsien government officials and of the inspired and trained populace. For a nation that sadly lacks military weapons, the cooperation of the people is of tremendous importance. If we had had three years instead of one we should have been able to make a good demonstration of what a modern local government ought to be on a province-wide scale. We did not complete it, but we know how it ought to be done. When the opportunity comes again, we will finish the job.

"By the way, recently, Dr. Robert Lim who did such outstanding medical and health work with the Chinese army, told me something that was very encouraging. He said when he faced the overwhelming responsibility of having to give medical service to such large numbers of troops with a dearth of trained personnel, he hardly knew how to start. This is what he said: 'One reason why I have been able to do it is that I've learned from the Tinghsien Health System the whole technique of passing on from the village Health Worker to the Sub-Hsien Health Station, and from that to the Hsien Health Center.'

"This system was so well adapted to the conditions of our people that on the recommendation of the Minister of Public Health, it was adopted by the Central Government and is now in operation in Free China. In my own province of Szechwan, Dr. C. C. Chen, who is now Commissioner of Public Health, was the one who conducted the health experiment in Tinghsien. In three years' time his staff has been increased from thirty to over eighteen hundred and his budget from $200,000, Chinese currency, to $20,000,-000. That gives you some idea of how constructive work goes on in China even in the midst of this war. It also shows that the Tinghsien Experiment persists in the life of the nation, even though Tinghsien is invaded by the enemy."

THE COLLEGE OF RURAL RECONSTRUCTION

"How can you carry out this enormous program without more leaders?" I inquired.

"I wonder if you know," he replied, "about the College of Rural Reconstruction which we established for this program. In the midst of wanton destruction and bombings by the enemy we started the National College of Rural Reconstruction in

November, 1940, near Chungking. Once it was known that the Mass Education Movement had established a college to train men and women for rural reconstruction, all the provincial governments of Free China, one after another, sent contributions ranging from ten to fifty thousand dollars each for the support of the college. My colleagues and I were greatly heartened by this expression, for nearly all the provincial treasuries were practically drained dry by the war. The chairman of our college Board is Governor Chang Chun. He is one of our ablest statesmen and a staunch supporter of all progressive movements in China. He was vice-president of the Executive Yuan at Nanking, and is now governor of Szechwan Province. The next important step is to deepen and broaden the basis of the College so that it will be adequately staffed and equipped to prepare competent leadership to meet the great demands of postwar reconstruction."

We sat silent for a few minutes, he seeming to forget where we were. His mind was ranging somewhere in the past, I supposed, over the twenty-five years he had spent among the millions of his own countrymen. He had done what he had set himself to do, those years ago, when as a young intellectual he saw and loved the poor, the illiterate, the diseased and oppressed among the common folk of his own land.

LEVELING UP

But I was entirely wrong, James Yen was not thinking of China and his own, nor of the past. He was thinking ahead, he was dreaming of the world.

"We talk a great deal these days about all kinds of world schemes," he said emphatically. "Now we have three-fourths of the world's population illiterate, under-fed, poorly clothed, badly sheltered, diseased and sorrowful. We all want a better world. But what do we really mean? What is the most basic element in the world? It's gold? It's iron? No, it's *people!* When we say a better world, we really mean we want better people.

"The basic problems of the three-fourths are what we have been discussing: illiteracy, poverty, disease and misgovernment. Look at the one billion people living in Asia. Easily 80 per cent of them are illiterate, poor, diseased and at the mercy of bad government.

"But, as I said before, any people in any part of the world, is entitled to at least a minimum of education, a minimum of livelihood, a minimum of health, and self-rule. Let's make the world's foundation, the people, broad and sound. Then, we'll have a better chance to build a better world. I do not believe in the leveling down of the one-fourth but the leveling up of the three-fourths.

"World council, world court, and an international

police force have their important place. But these international political organizations are only super-structures. They must be built on something in the minds and hearts of the people backed by the intelligence and conscience of the great masses of the world's peoples. Otherwise they are doomed to fail as they failed before. Mobilize the one-fourth to 'level up' the three-fourths!

"Some perhaps would object that this business of 'leveling up' the three-fourths is too fantastic—it involves too big an expense and too much sacrifice. But think of how much the Allies are spending for this war! The United States alone is spending $10,-300,000 per hour! When I was discussing this with President McCracken of Vassar, he asked me how much it cost to teach 47 million Chinese to read. I told him that the Chinese government spent an average of a dollar to teach an illiterate, approximately a total of $47,000,000. He said: 'That's about the amount we spend on the war in five hours.'

"As for human lives, which cannot be measured in dollars and cents, millions of combatants and many more millions of civilians—men, women and children—have been sacrificed. Apart from anything else, it is a simple matter of collective security.

"The 'have' people and the 'have' nations must realize that they are not safe unless the 'have not' people and the 'have not' nations too are satisfied. Call it enlightened self-interest if you will. Really, enlightened nationalism is internationalism. Your own country is only secure when others do not envy you. You can only be sure of your own bread when there are no starving people around you. I think that the idea and ideal of building up collective security and collective prosperity is the only sound one now. No nation today is secure alone, no nation is even healthy alone, because the diseases and germs of other nations will be brought there, too. This perhaps is the most potent motive for world reconstruction. The majority of people must be appealed to on the plane of self-interest. There are a few who can be reached on a higher plane, but not many.

"Still others might object that this process of leveling up the three-fourths would take too long. Perhaps so, but it can be shortened and accelerated. Few of us realize that there are approximately 300 million youths—of the teen-age—among the submerged peoples of the world who have never been exposed to any formal education. This presents a tremendous problem, but at the same time offers a vast opportunity for building a better world. Why? Non-education is better by far than mis-education. These unschooled youths, 300 million strong, represent a kind of blank sheet on which may be written the charter of a new world. The old ones are too old and the young ones are too young to take an active part in the world's reconstruction. Time *is* pressing. Let's put our major emphasis upon the training of this strategic group and use them as a *spearhead* for world reconstruction and world peace."

A GREAT QUESTION

Remembering the many Americans I knew who declare that they are not interested in other peoples until their own are made comfortable, I asked a question of James Yen as a Chinese. "Do you feel, as so many Americans do, that you should first get your own house in order—first make China perfect, so to speak, before you go to other countries?"

"My answer is both yes and no," he replied seriously. "Yes because our first responsibility is to our own people. No, because these problems are not peculiar to the people of China but are common to the three-fourths of the peoples of the world. It would be 'plain dumb' for each nation to tackle these basic common problems as 'isolationists.' A big job must be done in a big way. To start with, we may use one or two nations as a 'social laboratory' for the others, but the whole program must be later tackled on a world-wide scale. It will then generate world consciousness and a sense of global responsibility."

He stood up and faced me and I saw his eyes harden and shine. A great question was gathering in his mind. It was not me he faced, not to me he put the question. He was facing the world, and of the world he asked, "Why shouldn't we in every country who believe in these things band together as allies and fight against our common foes? Illiteracy, poverty, disease and mis-government—these are the enemies of all mankind. If everywhere at the same time we worked together against them, cooperatively and simultaneously, we could pool all our resources, we would encourage one another as we worked, we could work better, and we would the sooner reach our common goal."

He lifted his head and saw the vision, and the look in his eyes made me see it.

"Why not?" he asked.

I put the question to the world for answer. Why should we not band together everywhere, in every country, and fight our common foes, illiteracy poverty, disease and mis-government? The technique is here, the need is everywhere in terrifying measure.

"Why not?"

I hear the question from the peoples, not echo but demand.

EPILOGUE

YEARS HAVE PASSED since I wrote this little book. War has come and gone, leaving an uneasy peace. There have been many changes in the world. Countries in Asia that once were colonies are now independent nations. The mainland of China is under Communist domination.

One day in the fall of 1951, in the midst of all this, James Yen sat in an office in New York City with the American friends and supporters of the Mass Education Movement. The question we discussed was a large one. He put it to us frankly:

"Do you think our 30 years of experience in China might be helpful to other underdeveloped peoples?"

We all felt strongly that more than ever Asia needs rural reconstruction under trained leadership, and we agreed that James Yen should make an exploratory trip first to Asia to see whether this program, developed on Asian soil, could help other peoples of the underdeveloped countries, and to study the possibility of eventually establishing an international center of rural reconstruction where leaders could be trained for cooperating countries.

There was already precedent for such a center. Even during the war in China the Movement founded, in the midst of Japanese invasion, the College of Rural Reconstruction in Szechwan Province, which I touched upon briefly before. The College was unique in that it was the first and only experimental college in China. Revolutionary in concept, its curriculum, unlike any existing college, was adapted to the needs of rural people, and the teachings of the classroom were directly related to actual field practice. This drastic departure from the orthodox met with strong opposition at the beginning by the Ministry of Education. Later, seeing the effectiveness of the College's new approach in training young people for rural service, the Ministry modified its attitude and accepted the College as a fully accredited institution of higher education.

It would be well for me to pause here to emphasize the fact that the Movement had not only developed an effective system of mass education and rural reconstruction for the common people, but also made a profound impact upon higher education in China. For example, a project of great educational significance was the organization of the North China Council of Rural Reconstruction whose specific aim was to revitalize higher education, making it better adapted to the needs of China which has a predominantly rural population. The universities that participated in the Council were Yenching (for sociology), Tsinghwa (for sanitary engineering), Nankai (for political science), Nanking (for agriculture), and Peking Union Medical College (for public health). One concrete result of the Council's efforts was the establishment of a new Medical School, giving equal importance to the training of students for curative and preventive medicine. Other schools, such as education, local government, were to follow but had to be given up because of the widespread devastation caused by the Japanese invasion.

The impact of the Movement was not confined to institutions in China. Many organizations abroad also were benefited by its program and techniques. For example, when the United Nations Educational, Scientific and Cultural Organization (Unesco) was first set up, the Mass Education Movement was invited to assist it in formulating its Fundamental Education Program. Dr. Ch'u Shih-yin, the Movement's representative, attended the first Unesco conference held in Paris, November 1945, and made valuable contributions.

Then in 1947, James Yen was asked to head Unesco's Fundamental Education Program. In his invitation to James Yen, Dr. Julian Huxley, the then Director-General cabled thus: ". . . hope you may feel this might offer scope for extending your great work in China to world-wide field." Though James Yen was not able to accept the invitation because of his responsibilities in China, he nevertheless continued to give assistance to Unesco from time to time as Consultant.

The Movement also played a vital part in bringing into being the Chinese-American Joint Commission on Rural Reconstruction (JCRR). The JCRR had been cited as a model for joint cooperation in U. S. foreign aid. But few realized that it was James Yen who sparked the idea of the JCRR, or that in the Congressional Records, it was referred to as the "Jimmy Yen Provision." The story follows.

When the war with Japan was over, James Yen had hoped that this rice-roots program of mass education and rural reconstruction could be applied to the whole of China, for it was generally agreed that this was the answer to the desperate needs of a people physically and spiritually exhausted after twenty-odd years of civil war and eight years of foreign war. But peace and reconstruction was not in sight. Communist forces began moving across the land. The Government had to concentrate its resources upon fighting them. Seeing how grave the situation was, James Yen came to the United States in 1947, and, with the help of American friends, sought U. S. aid to reach where it was most needed—the Chinese masses. He saw and talked with many friends in and outside the U. S. Government about his plan.

Among them was General George C. Marshall, then Secretary of State, who had just returned from China. At his suggestion, James Yen sent him a memorandum, the gist of which was that the Economic and Social Front was just as important as the Military Front; that the rice-field was even more vital than the battlefield. Unless top priority was given to meet the desperate needs of the poverty-stricken masses, we would certainly lose the "min-shin"—the heart of the people. This was followed by a concrete program of mass education and rural reconstruction to improve the conditions of the rural people and to strengthen the Economic and Social Front.

James Yen also saw President Harry S. Truman. The President said that he was interested in helping the Chinese Government, but he was even more interested in helping the *people* of China. This was exactly what Yen's plan proposed to do. Yen explained to the President that while his program would be concerned with the welfare of millions of people, especially the peasants, it would cost only a modest amount of money; and that it would not be a program of relief, but of *release*—release of the potential powers of the people for production, reconstruction and democratic citizenship. Then he suggested that a Joint Commission on Rural Reconstruction consisting of both American and Chinese members be organized to administer the program. The President was greatly impressed with Yen's plan and gave it his whole-hearted support.

Well-known newspapers such as the New York Herald Tribune, the Christian Science Monitor, the Washington Post published editorials endorsing James Yen's program. The result was that when Congress passed the China Aid Act for 1948, it provided that up to 10 per cent of the appropriation of $275,000,000 be earmarked for rural reconstruction, and that a Joint Commission on Rural Reconstruction (JCRR) be formed to administer the program. There were five members on the Commission, three Chinese and two Americans, appointed by the Presidents of their respective governments, and James Yen was one of the members.

The JCRR was able to operate for only sixteen months before the Communists took over Mainland China. It spent only about $4,000,000 of its allotment of $27,500,000. Yet its projects of agriculture, irrigation, cooperative organization, public health, literacy, and land-tenure reform reached an estimated 60,000,-000 Chinese peasants. It was said to be the most successful foreign aid program ever launched by the United States for China.

Paul Hoffman, first ECA Administrator, emphasized the significance of this educational achievement in his article, "The Most Courageous Comeback in History" (LIFE, February 5, 1951). He wrote: "In the very provinces where the JCRR program had got underway—in Szechuan, Kwangsi and Fukien—the Communist invaders found some of the most stubborn resistance to their drive. What a different story might have been told in China if this alternative to Communist strategy had been started a few years earlier."

In similar words, Justice William O. Douglas of the U. S. Supreme Court stated in his book *North from Malaya*, that had this program "been started a decade or even five years earlier, it might easily have become the counterrevolution that would have swept Communism aside."

While it was regrettable that the JCRR was not able to carry on its program on the mainland, what it was able to accomplish in such a short time showed what could be done on a large scale elsewhere—in other underdeveloped countries.

We friends of the Mass Education Movement firmly believed that this China experience of thirty years in mass education and rural reconstruction should be of great value to other underdeveloped peoples who are confronted with similar basic problems. Furthermore, many leaders in Asia, noting the practicality and effectiveness of the Movement's program in China, saw it as the answer to the needs of their people. The program was Asian in origin, developed by and for Asians, to meet realistically the basic needs of the Asian peasant. As a result of many meetings with James Yen, we decided in 1951 to organize the International Mass Education Movement

(IMEM) to make this program available to them.

In February 1952, James Yen went on behalf of the IMEM to visit the leading Asian countries to get first-hand information about what other agencies, government and private, were doing to help the rural people. At the same time, he was to find out whether any country would be interested in welcoming IMEM's cooperation in starting a rural reconstruction program.

During his trip an interesting incident happened, which showed the far-reaching influence of the Movement's program. When James Yen was in India, he heard about a fine rural development project being carried out in Etawah in Uttar Pradesh Province, and went to see it. This was the project that was being used as a pattern for the Community Development Program of India's Five Year Plan. When the workers heard of James Yen's coming, they were eager to meet him and to discuss their problems with him. To his surprise and delight, he learned that this book *Tell The People* was a great help and inspiration to them. One of the dedicated young Indian leaders in the Etawah project, Mr. Baij Nath Singh, told him that he used it as his "Bible" for rural reconstruction.

Many of the countries James Yen visited were anxious to get IMEM's cooperation, but he was most interested in the Philippines because of the moving response of the local civic leaders, whom he called "kindred spirits." Inspired by his story of the Movement's work in China, they organized the Philippine Rural Reconstruction Movement (PRRM) to carry out a similar program to raise the economic and social standard of their village people. Eager to be benefited by the China experience, the PRRM asked for IMEM's cooperation and assistance, and invited James Yen to be their Adviser.

The PRRM, a civic, indigenous movement, has on its Board some of the nation's outstanding leaders representing education, business, industry, banking, and social welfare. Although the country is predominantly Catholic, the PRRM is non-sectarian. Catholics, Protestants and Buddhists serve on its national Board, banding themselves together to help their underprivileged countrymen in the villages. The staff of the PRRM is 100 per cent Filipino, from the President to the village worker.

Using the China program as a guide, the PRRM set up two pilot centers, one in the province of Nueva Ecija and the other in Rizal. While its experiments and demonstrations have been, necessarily, of a qualitative character confined to a few areas, its influence has been nation-wide. Today, the PRRM can point proudly to an impressive record of achievement. The following are a few examples.

It has created a new profession for college youths and set a pattern for rural reconstruction training. For some time, people had thought that rural reconstruction could be undertaken by village school teachers or social workers during their leisure hours. But rural reconstruction is a gigantic and difficult task, involving millions of people. It demands full-time, well-trained and dedicated workers.

In order to demonstrate the necessity and value of training such workers, the PRRM decided in 1953 to tap a source of manpower, hitherto untapped, namely, the college-educated youths of the land. When the idea was first brought up, many friends were skeptical about it, because college graduates, they argued, wanted only white-collar jobs, not work in the poor, backward villages. Members of the PRRM, however, went to work; they visited the colleges in the country, gave talks to the students, and pointed out to them the urgency and importance of helping to solve the problems facing their own people in the villages. Then they challenged these youths to join the PRRM to serve as rural reconstruction workers to their neglected countrymen and to help build their nation from the foundation, the villages.

To the surprise of all, hundreds of students responded! They were put through six months of rigorous training in the villages where they lived and worked with the villagers and learned the techniques of rural reconstruction. More importantly, their intimate association with the peasants gave them an understanding of the age-old problems and handicaps of the illiterate and disinherited. Those who survived the hardships of the course—and only about 50 per cent did—have proved to be competent and dedicated workers.

In his comment on the PRRM's training program, Mr. Miguel Gaffud, a leading Filipino educator and government official, wrote in his booklet entitled *Public and Private Agencies of Community Development*:

"One civic organization that has distinguished itself in evolving definite patterns in the uplift of village life is the Philippine Rural Reconstruction Movement (PRRM) . . . The significant achievement of the PRRM is not in its coverage but it has proved that any program of community development requires special training of personnel and that these workers must live with the people of the village. These principles of personnel training and living with the village folks are the two principles being followed in the implementation of the activities of the Presidential Assistant of Community Development."

The late President Ramon Magsaysay of the Philippines was able to see for himself the effective job the PRRM was doing in training college students for rural work, when he was invited to speak at the graduation exercises of its first group of trainees, held in 1954 in Galvan, Guimba, Nueva Ecija. He was deeply impressed with the practical projects done there by these college young men and women during their period of training, especially with their *spirit of dedication* and willingness to live in the villages and their ability to identify themselves with the life of the humble village folks. Shortly afterwards, President Magsaysay asked the PRRM to take charge of his San Luis Project in the province of Pampanga which was for resettling the villagers who had been driven out of San Luis by the "Huks" (local communists.)

Another significant contribution that the PRRM has made to the nation is its pioneering work in self-government at the village level. Being an indigenous movement, a movement for the Filipino people and by the Filipino people, the PRRM was in a position to undertake this important phase of its four-fold integrated program, namely, self-government.

The old laws of the Philippines specified that every village should have a village council, but few villages ever organized one. In the few that did exist, the members were appointed by their county councilors. However, in the PRRM pilot centers, the PRRM set up, side by side with its projects in agriculture, health and education, field experiments to train the people for village self-government. Simultaneously, in Manila, the PRRM conducted a village self-government forum to which government officials and specialists in local government were invited. Members of the Philippine Congress were also urged to see first-hand the self-government projects in the PRRM pilot areas. Through the actual experimentation in the villages and these forum discussions, great interest was generated.

As a result, in the summer of 1955, a bill was intro-

duced in the Philippine Congress under the leadership
of a member of the PRRM Board, the late Senator
Tomas Cabili, to make all village councils in the
Philippines elective. It was passed by both Houses
and signed by President Magsaysay, and became Republic Act 1245.

Following the PRRM pattern of the four-fold program, each village under the new Village Council
Law now elects a councilor respectively for education, livelihood, and health. The fourth phase of the
PRRM program, self-government, is represented in
itself by the Village Council. The first national elec-
tion of village councilors in Philippine history was
held on January 17, 1956.

From the foregoing summary of the work of the
International Mass Education Movement, two salient
points emerge: (1) the applicability of the basic principles and techniques of the China program to another
Asian country, and (2) the vital part of a civic and
indigenous movement in the rural reconstruction program of an underdeveloped country.

This down-to-earth program, as promoted by the
International Mass Education Movement and demonstrated by the PRRM (a civic and indigenous movement) is one that appeals to the civic-spirited, democratic elements of the community, and rallies them
together to work for their underprivileged countrymen, despite their differences in religion and political

555039148

affiliations. It is a program that challenges the ideal-
ism of the college students, the educated youths who
are the "wave of the future," and impels them to offer
themselves as village workers, rural reconstruction
"missionaries." Above all, it is a program that has
proved its effectiveness in training the village people
to *fight against hunger and disease and to develop self-
reliance and self-government.*

THE INTERNATIONAL INSTITUTE OF
RURAL RECONSTRUCTION

Inspired by the significant results achieved by the
Movement to date, and hopeful of the great contribution it should make to other underdeveloped countries, the Board members of the International Mass
Education Movement has decided to establish the International Institute of Rural Reconstruction in the
Philippines for the following purposes:

1) To train qualified young men and women from
   cooperating underdeveloped countries in the fundamental principles and practices of mass education and rural reconstruction so as the equip them
   technically and spiritually to undertake the
   mission of training their own people to fight
   against hunger and disease and to develop self-
   reliance and self-government;

2) To gather together a nucleus of creative and dedicated teachers (scientists and scholars) of world
   outlook who are not only technically competent
   but spiritually capable of inspiring their students;

3) To extend, upon invitation, the rural reconstruction program to cooperating underdeveloped countries by assisting their nationals to organize indigenous and civic rural reconstruction movements;

4) To conduct field research and experimentation (regionally, nationally, internationally) in order to evolve and continue to improve theories and practices of rural reconstruction; to produce the basic materials for same; and to serve as a clearing house for information and data.

This is a monumental undertaking. The rightness of the undertaking and the practical plans James Yen and his colleagues have drawn up are convincing indeed. Victor Hugo said: "Nothing in the world is so powerful as an idea whose time has come." The time of mass education and rural reconstruction *has* come. We must press on with greater zeal and determination.

New York City
April 1959